Prevent Doomsday
An Anti Nuclear Anthology

Table Of Contents

I   Introduction

by Vinson Brown

"He shall judge between the nations, and shall rebuke all peoples; and they shall beat swords into ploughshares, and their spears into pruning hooks. Nation shall not lift up sword against nation; neither shall they make war anymore! Isaiah 3:4."

Regardless of whether we believe in a Supreme Being or not, it would be incredible to me if any intelligent person would deny that the above words show great wisdom and are exactly what the world needs in this age of nuclear terror. This is both a stern command and a wonderful promise to all of us to get busy and fulfill our true destiny. If we fail in the job, we fail the billions of children on this earth and all the generations to come. The alternative, Nuclear War, is so horrible, so completely devastating that it is sickening that any persons would actually contemplate using these incredible weapons that will wipe out whole nations almost with one blow.

This does not mean the writers of the essays in this book advocate unilateral disarmament, or our country disarming while other countries continue with their armaments. These thoughts and ideas are given to us by mature men and women, scientists, writers, diplomats, philosophers, who see the present catastrophic destruction promised by a nuclear war, and wish to show us ways to peace and harmony between nations.

The second essay, by Dr. James E. Muller of Harvard Medical School warns us of the great danger of Accidental Nuclear War. Dr. Muller, the founder of International Physicians for Prevention of a Nuclear War, explains how easily a human being, flawed by alcohol or drugs or other influences, might bring about a nuclear explosion that would start a total war. Knowing this danger should make all of us anxious to see the world brought back to sanity.

The third essay, by Vinson Brown, natural science author and publisher, *Three Beginning Steps to World Peace*, draws on the vital experiences of General Douglas MacArthur as Allied Commissioner of Japan immediately after World War II, and on Warren Christopher, former Assistant Secretary of State and one of the diplomats in Algiers who helped engineer the release of the hostages from Iran, to show us these needed steps to peace. Both of these men used a standard of intelligence, calmness and patience to establish their victories. We need more of this in the present world.

The fourth essay, *The Peace Corps: Making Friends for America*, by Landrum R. Bolling, from an article in the *Saturday Evening Post*, gives us a clear view of one way America is already working towards peace by helping the poor people of other nations become self-sufficient and self-reliant, a step that needs to be much more widespread. Vinson Brown adds an addenda on this last subject.

The fifth essay, by Donald Keys, the President of Planetary Citizens, on *The Healing of the Nations*, gives us a grand view of how the United Nations, despite difficulties and failures, is working to create a better and more harmonious world by healing the nations.

The sixth essay, by Muriel Ferguson, *The Whole Earth Conspiracy*, author of the famous book, *The Aquarian Conspiracy*, speaks of unity on the people level, but thrillingly explains it from the standpoint of a very wise woman and with interesting examples of how it is happening to many nationalities.

The seventh essay, *Peace as a Paradigm Shift*, by Michael N. Nagler, associate professor of Classics and Comparative Literature at the University of California in Berkeley, gives us in brilliant language how peoples and nations need to move out of the now fatal paradigm of war-mindedness into the new and far more mature idea of the brotherhood of all mankind.

The eighth essay, *Cease This Madness*, by George Kennan, former Ambassador to Russia for many years, gives us a look at the terrifying lack of understanding between the two superpowers, the USA and the USSR, caused mainly by illogical prejudices, that could lead one or the other to make a fatal mistake that would trigger World War III. It urges both to "cease this madness" and begin to work together for more understanding and eventual world peace.

The ninth essay, *Compassion, Science and World Peace*, by Vinson Brown, shows how we can combine our compassion for the children and indeed for all life on this planet with the scientific method to bring peace. To do so, he says, science must be used by our leaders in the fullest and most mature sense of the word, considering intelligently and equally diligently all possible alternatives on the road to peace, avoiding bickering, namecalling and futile arguments, in a high-level endeavor to create a world community where all nations are given secure protection against war under world law.

The tenth essay, by Dr. Louis Rene Beres, *Steps Towards a New Planetary Identity*, passionately calls for a reorienting of our thinking so that the nationalism of modern nations can begin to merge into a new planetary consciousness and cooperation that will eliminate war. Dr. Beres was one of the ten finalists in the 1980 Rabinowich International Essay Competition, and is the author or co-author of several books dealing with world peace.

The eleventh essay, by Dr. Roger Fisher of Harvard School of Law, *The Nuclear Solution, Giving up the Plutonium Security Blanket*, delights us humorously but warns us seriously by showing how human beings allow themselves to drift toward war, and how we can change this drift the other way. Dr. Fisher's new book on *Getting To Yes, Negotiating Agreement Without Giving In*, should be read in conjunction with this book to show how we can intelligently and maturely negotiate with other nations the roads that lead to World Peace.

The last essay by Vinson Brown, on *Let's Negotiate The Peace Of The World*, gives some examples of the actual negotiating steps that are needed to bring first Russia and America, and then the rest of the world, into a harmonious plan and organization for world peace.

II   On Accidental Nuclear War

by James E. Muller

When the horror of nuclear war forces its way to consciousness, many cling to the belief that it is so horrible that no rational person will ever push the button. This discounts our stated policy that we would push the button in self-defense, but it does provide comfort — until the possibility of accidental nuclear war is considered.

The military, to whom we have delegated the task of managing nuclear weapons, well understands the danger of unintentional nuclear war. A special program called the Personnel Reliability Program (PRP) exists for individuals with access to nuclear weapons. More than 100,000 are included in the program; to enter it, an individual must show evidence of emotional stability and good social adjustment and not have had a problem with alcohol or drug abuse. Physicians assist in the screening process and periodically monitor those selected.

The results of this surveillance are shocking. They should be known by everyone who believes nuclear weapons bring national security, every world leader, every arms-control negotiator — indeed, everyone living in the nuclear age — yet it seems very few are aware of the numbers buried on page 323 of the 1979 report of "Hearings Before a Subcommittee of the Committee on Appropriations of the House of Representatives." In 1975, 5,128 personnel were removed from access to nuclear weapons because of violations of the PRP; in 1976, 4,966 and in 1977, 4,973 — an annual rate exceeding 4 percent. Reasons for removal in 1977 included alcohol and drug abuse; the primary drug abused was marijuana, but more than 250 were removed for abuse of drugs such as heroin and LSD. In the same year 1,289 were removed for a "significant physical, mental or character trait or aberrant behavior, substantiated by competent medical authority," which might "prejudice reliable performance of the duties of a particular critical or controlled position."

Misconduct: In addition to these medical disqualifications, 828 were disqualified for negligence, 350 for court-martial or civil convictions of a serious nature and 885 for evidence "of a contemptuous attitude toward the law." Description of this misconduct should not be interpreted as a criticism of the military, for it is we who have asked them to accomplish the impossible in handling nuclear weapons safely.

Computers, which occasionally tell us we have died, or never existed, or must pay a bill a second time, are also intimately involved in the nuclear arsenals. The record of mistakes is extensive. During an eighteen-month period, the North American Air Defense Command had 151 false alarms. Four resulted in orders that increased the state of alert of B-52 bomber crews and intercontinental-ballistic-missile units. A major false alert lasting a full six minutes, occurred when a technician mistakenly mounted on an American military computer a training tape of a Soviet attack. Mechanical malfunction and human errors have also led to a number of accidents with nuclear weapons.

The risk of an accident increases as we increase the size of our arsenal and the number of personnel involved. Our move to "counterforce" warfare, in which each side becomes concerned that it must fire its missiles before they are destroyed, decreases to less than 30 minutes the time available to evaluate the computer signals of a possible attack and decide to launch. The spread of nuclear weapons to less-developed countries with limited technical sophistication also increases the risk.

What are the implications of this understandable but somehow startling evidence of technical and human fallibility? Can a group of individuals whose judgment is impaired decide to launch a nuclear weapon without authorization or fail to respond properly to a computer error? Although the Pentagon has stated that no single person can launch a nuclear weapon, under certain conditions the crew of a submarine can fire nuclear weapons on its own. Our survival also depends on the proper conduct of Soviet personnel and computers. Alcoholism is a major health problem in the Soviet Union and is at least as likely to exist among their military as it is among ours.

An unauthorized launch would undoubtedly require a combination of failures, but the opportunities are numerous and increasing. Must we drift passively toward that moment when chance brings together the critical mass of plutonium and drugs, alcohol, psychosis or computer error that will destroy us and all we value?

Disaster: We are moving inexorably and unwittingly toward a finale similar to that so powerfully described in "Hamlet." At the play's conclusion, Fortinbras enters and finds the recently slain Hamlet, Laertes and the King and Queen of Denmark, and Hamlet's friend Horatio explains how such a disaster occurred:

And let me speak to th' yet unknowing world
How these things came about. So shall you hear
Of carnal, bloody and unnatural acts,
Of accidental judgments, casual slaughters,
Of deaths put on by cunning and forced cause,
And, in this upshot, purposes mistook
Fall'n on th' inventors' heads.

We are now the "inventors." We have set the stage for "accidental judgments," "forced cause" and "purposes mistook" to lead us, not to a series of palace murders, but to an event of unimaginable horror in which millions of innocent people will die agonizing deaths. Physicians who survive will be unable to provide even minimal pain relief for most of the dying.

There is really only one cause for optimism: the phenomenal growth of the mass movement for total nuclear disarmament. Hope and a sense of common purpose have replaced despair and isolation for tens of thousands. If others with similar concerns act on their belief, the movement can become an unstoppable force. The coming spring can be a time of renewal of belief that humanity can survive. Such progress is needed: the hour is late. We can live with the threat of accidental nuclear war for 10 or 20 or 30 years, as we have — but not forever.

* * *

Note: Dr. Muller teaches at the Harvard Medical School and is a founder of International Physicians for Prevention of Nuclear War. His article was published in the March 1, 1982 issue of Newsweek, reproduced here by kind permission of Newsweek.

III Three Beginning Steps To World Peace

by Vinson Brown

The Terrible Problem

"You are an adult living in a time when the leaders of the world are behaving like little children; where the theme of the day is a terrorist one, humane concerns inhumanely expressed."[1]

"As a nation we have developed a dangerously short attention span. We turn expectantly from one media event to another. We want entertainment, not enlightenment. We can't seem to concentrate on the abiding question of what our humanity requires of each of us: (to choose between world destruction or world peace)"[2]

This is the major challenge of our age which none of us can any longer ignore. Are we to drift into a war more horrible than we can imagine, as stupid an end to this creation as men can devise? And where are the grownup human beings like General Omar Bradley of World War II who said:"The difficult we do right away; the impossible takes a little time!"

We must get out of our dream world and into the action. To create World Peace is NOT an impossible dream! It takes effort and a little time! The stakes are the most tremendous in history. Mankind is now spending hundreds of billions of dollars on terrible weapons of mass destruction, billions that could be spent on health, education, arts and crafts, and many other humane efforts for the well-being of all of us that are desperately needed. When will we stop this madness?

Proposed here are THREE GIANT STEPS TO WORLD PEACE. There are other steps we can take also, but these three would certainly be a good beginning. "A world with the capacity for the ultimate crime of total genocide ought not to hesitate too long before renouncing that fatal course."[3]

Step Number One — Peace through Understanding

First let us go back to a time about thirty-five years ago to see what one man was able to do for peace between nations and so understand steps we need to take on a larger scale today.

In September 1945 there was standing on the deck of the mighty battleship Missouri in Yokahama Harbor near Tokyo, Japan, a man who would show two ways of creative harmony between nations. Though his genius and brilliance would later be marred by some serious mistakes of the ego, the task he set for himself and Japan to do in the years from 1945 to 1950 was a supreme example of human intelligence acting at its best and highest.

The man was General of the Armies, Douglas MacArthur, and the nation Japan, a people crushed and broken by overwhelming force into hopelessness and despair. Almost alone among all the generals, admirals and diplomats of America and the other Allied nations that stood on the deck of the warship Missouri that fateful September 2, 1945, General Douglas MacArthur faced the Japanese officials, come to sign the Treaty of Peace that would end World War II, with friendly eyes. Most of the others threw looks at the Japanese that blazed with hostility and scorn. As one of the Japanese leaders, Toshukase Kasa, wrote later:

"A million eyes seemed to beat on us with millions of shafts of a rattling storm of arrows barbed with fire. I felt their keeness sink into my body with a sharp physical pain. Never had I realized that the glance of glaring eyes could hurt me so much. We watched —standing in the public gaze like penitent boys awaiting the dreaded schoolmaster. I tried to preserve the dignity of defeat, but it was difficult and every minute contained ages!"[4]

But one man alone changed all this by his words. Standing against the tide of hate like Lincoln when he gave the Gettysburg Address, General Douglas MacArthur presented a similarly remarkable speech:

"We are gathered here, representatives of the major warring powers, to conclude a solemn agreement whereby peace may be restored. —We must not meet in a spirit of distrust, malice, or hatred. —Instead, both sides must rise to that higher dignity which alone benefits the sacred purposes we are about to serve. It is my earnest hope, and indeed the hope of all mankind, that a better world shall emerge, a world founded upon faith and understanding — a world dedicated to the dignity of man and the fulfillment of his most cherished wish, — for freedom, tolerance and justice."[5]

Toshukase Kase was shaken deeply by these sonorous words. He wrote: "What stirring eloquence and what a noble vision! Here is the victor announcing the verdict to the prostrate enemy. He can exact his pound of flesh if he chooses. He can impose a humiliating penalty if he so desires. And yet he pleads for freedom, tolerance, and justice. For me, who expected the worst humiliation, this was a complete surprise. I was thrilled beyond words, spellbound, thunderstruck. For the living heroes and dead martyrs of the war this speech was a wreath of undying flowers. MacArthur's words sailed on wings, so that this narrow quarterdeck was now transformed INTO AN ALTAR OF PEACE!"[6]

It is important to give here these reactions of a Japanese, for they soon reverberated from the hearts of almost an entire people. MacArthur became literally their hero, and, through his understanding of them, able to change the feelings of a nation from despair and bitterness, hate and prejudice, into thoughts of cooperation, trust and love.

Hirohito, the Emperor of Japan, MacArthur realized, was a key figure to be treated with respect and honor so that he could help in the job of reforming the nation. Many American generals and other officials had demanded the Emperor should be tried for war crimes, but MacArthur understood he had been mainly a puppet of his generals, and won his wholehearted cooperation in creating a peaceable Japan. Clearly MacArthur understood how to control and inspire the Japanese!

MacArthur also had another vital understanding. Despite the fact that he was a general, trained for warfare, he understood that wars had become so terrible that a world system to prevent them was now vital. In a speech, which was printed in the February, 1955 issue of Life Magazine, MacArthur drove right to the heart of our present terrifying dilemma.

"At the turn of the century, when I entered the army, the target was one enemy casualty at the end of a rifle or bayonet or sword.

Then came the machine gun, designed to kill by the dozen. After that — the heavy artillery gun, gaining death by the hundreds. Then the aerial bomb, to strike down the thousands, followed by the atomic explosion to reach the hundreds of thousands. Now, electronics and other processes of science have raised the destructive potential to encompass millions. And with restless hands we work feverishly in dark laboratories to find the means to destroy all in one blow. This very triumph of scientific annihilation destroys the possibility of war being a medium of practical settlement of international differences. — No longer does it possess the choice of the winner of a duel — it contains rather the germs of double suicide!"[7]

Understanding our enemies and understanding our friends, plus understanding the fearful choice we face of completely destructive war or peace, are basic to our taking the necessary steps to end war.

Step Number Two — Winning the Masses of the World

In Japan MacArthur showed us how to do this. His gentle and courteous treatment of the Emperor won countless hearts, as did his strict rule to his military police to make sure American servicemen treated the Japanese, and particularly the women, with respect and courtesy. American soldiers and sailors did many kind deeds for the people and their children that helped win more millions to friendship in the defeated land.

When MacArthur, as Administrator of the Peace in Japan after the war, taught the Japanese the ways of freedom of speech and press, equality of women in the vote, and justice to the farmers by arranging to give these severely exploited tillers of the soil a way to own their own lands, he inspired much delight and friendship. But when he went so far as to establish free unions for the workers, and curbed the powers of the big corporations so that the smaller business people could develop their ideas and businesses without being monopolized out of existence, the people of Japan were thrilled and moved deeply.

By assisting the underprivileged to win rights that raised them economically MacArthur won a battle against Communism in

Japan that could not have been duplicated by a thousand armored regiments! Wherever Communism has been successful in winning converts it has been in countries where the common people were being heavily exploited by the rich and the politicians. This exploitation is not a sign of true conservatism but exactly the opposite, an open invitation to subversion, violence and revolution!

Our corporations of all sizes, who send representatives and branches to foreign lands, have tremendous possibilities and responsibilities for their own interest to help the common people help themselves become creative and self-supporting, so improving their economic and social standing. Far more profits will come in the long run to those corporations who win friends in such a way, which also will blunt and finally destroy subversive efforts to take over such countries. We have some good examples of this kind of effort among a few corporations and in the efforts of the Peace Corps to help poor peoples around the world become self-supporting.

Our tourists who visit foreign lands can also be ambassadors of peace and good-will if they act with simple courtesy and kindness. I was able to make many friends among the Panamanians, in my two years visit there, only when I stopped looking down at them and began to see their good qualities.

Step Number Three — Winning Peace by Talking

It should be clear to all of us that intelligent communication between peoples to find ways of agreement and cooperation is a major step to world peace. I have been astonished by the apparent blindness of most of our leaders to quickly increase the ease of contact and understanding by working together through mutual agreement to establish a World Language. It could be either one of the present widely-used languages or an artificial language, like Esperanto or Interlingua. If school children everywhere began to study and learn this World Language, very soon we would be able to communicate between nations without all the pitfalls and difficulties in learning the talk of other peoples that we run into today. Too often, for example, a vital communication may be completely misunderstand when it is translated. What a blessing to real communication all over the earth such a World Language would be!

Meanwhile we have to talk as best we can through interpreters or through those few diplomats who speak several languages well. To keep the talking for peace going is vital, as has been proved in the past. Warren Christopher, who was one of the diplomats who kept the talks with the Iranians moving in Algeria until at last the American hostages were freed, put this better than I can in a Commencement Day Address he gave at Stanford University in May, 1981.

"We may come to think we can punish our adversaries by refusing to talk with them — or by our silence induce changes in policies we deplore. But, without talking, without diplomacy, an essential instrument of our national security is lost.

"Talking can also tame conflict, lift the human condition, and move us close to the ideal of peace. It implies direct communication, whether to define our views, to explain our actions, to win acceptance, or to invite cooperation. It involves addressing differences, struggling to identify them, and, ultimately, one hopes, to resolve them. Eric Severeid once defined talking as a way 'to seek a meeting of minds without a knocking together of heads.'

"Talking created our oldest and strongest alliance. Talking stopped the poisonous testing of nuclear weapons in the atmosphere. Talking unraveled decades of suspicion and hostility towards China. In the Middle East talking forged the first peace between Israel and Egypt.

"We and the Soviets, even when our differences are the sharpest, still have at least one common interest — the interest in survival. We have, therefore, a common need to talk, to seek dependable ways to avoid the conflagration that would consume both of us."

Surely, by the intelligent talking that Warren Christopher advocates, without name-calling, all people can be brought to see that war is death and peace is life, war is insanity and stupidity, while peace is wisdom and truth, war is darkness and peace is light!

Sources of Quotations

1 From DIG INTO THE WORLD, by Alan Alda.

2 From a speech of Senator Charles MacC. Mathias, Jr., at the University of Kansas, November 7, 1978. "Will the Cockroach Inherit the Earth?"

3 Ibid.

4 From AMERICAN CAESAR, Douglas MacArthur, 1880-1964, by William Manchester, 1978, Little, Brown & Co. pages 451-452.

5 Ibid. page 452.

6 Ibid. page 452.

7 From LIFE MAGAZINE, in a February, 1955 issue.

IVA The Peace Corps: Making Friends For America*

by Landrum R. Bolling

*The broad spirit of volunteerism of which
President Reagan speaks still "flows, as it has through our
nation's history, like a deep and mighty river."*

The proud wearer of a Peace Corps button braces for the barrage of questions it spontaneously inspires: "Peace Corps? Is it still alive? Is it still around?"

"How can this be?" asks Loret Miller Ruppe, Peace Corps director. 'How can Americans not know? Why aren't they given the opportunity to stand up and be proud of a government program that has tapped the spirit of America—that broad spirit of volunteerism of which President Reagan so often speaks, calling it 'A spirit that flows like a deep and mighty river through the history of our nations'? The spirit flows, but how? Where? Who has it?" And who had it?

For starters, of course, there are President Reagan and Director Ruppe. Then, John F. Kennedy. "Miss Lillian" Carter. Bill Moyers. The King of Tonga. Senator Paul Tsongas. Father Hesburgh. Sargent Shriver. Unlikely allies, but all linked through one strong common interest: the Peace Corps.

Shriver was the founding director of the Corps—which began in 1961—and served under his liberal Democrat brother-in-law, President Kennedy, who originally proposed the organization in his campaign promises. Loret Miller Ruppe, President Reagan's Peace Corps head, is—like her chief—a conservative Republican. Yet both directors testify to the enthusiastic backing of their chief executives, 20 years and political poles apart. Both directors won their White House standing through vigorous and successful election campaigning, Ruppe as cochairman of the Reagan-Bush team in Michigan.

Today, Ruppe has the formidable task of translating White House support into ongoing budgetary and fiscal policy decisions in a time of fiscal constraint and widespread American hostility to the Third World in general and, especially, to foreign aid. Nevertheless, she is confident that the Peace Corps is on the threshold of a new era of growth and public recognition, fully in harmony with President Reagan's philosophy of expanding the private-sector role in serving the public good. But it isn't easy, especially since the Peace Corps has had such a low profile in recent years that many people, even in government-centered Washington, assume that it was one to those "nice ideas" that was abandoned long ago. Fortunately, she has a diverse group of high-profile allies, many of whom know the Peace Corps from intimate experience. Paul Tsongas was just out of college when he volunteered to teach in a small-town school in Ethiopia in 1962. Two years later, he came home bent on pursuing a life of public service, his world view largely shaped by his experiences as a PC volunteer. Presently, four other members of Congress are alumni of the Peace Corps: Senator Christopher J. Dodd (D-CT), who once served in the Dominican Republic; members of the House, James A. Courter (R-NJ), who served in Venezuela; Thomas E. Petri (R-WI), who spent his two years in Somalia; and tony P. Hall (D-OH), who served in Thailand.

The Peace Corps was at its peak in funding and overseas representation and Lyndon Johnson was in the White House when, in 1966, Lillian Carter, past 60, signed up. She went off from her home in Plains, Georgia, to use her nursing skills to aid a village in India. More than a decade later, it seemed only proper that President Jimmy Carter should include his PC-volunteer mother in an official delegation that was sent to India.

The King of Tonga, ruler of a tiny island kingdom in the South Pacific, is representative of scores of other heads of state who, over the past two decades, have warmly welcomed and generously praised the volunteers the U.S. Peace Corps has sent out in successive waves to help with the grassroots problems of developing countries. Many of them want far more PCVs than the U.S. is able to send.

"Father Ted" Hesburgh, the internationalist, social-activist president of the University of Notre Dame, is hardly a typical Roman Catholic priest or college president, yet he symbolizes a considerable number of educators, religious leaders and other public-spirited citizens who have taken time off from regular duties to help with planning, training and field-review activities of the Peace Corps, particularly, as in his case, in Latin America.

Bill Moyers, before he became President Johnson's press secretary, served as a deputy director of the Peace Corps. That experience helped to strengthen his Southern Babtist idealism and broaden his understanding of the world. It helped shape his approach to his later career as one of the nation's leading media commentators on world affairs.

Over the past two decades, the Peace Corps has enlisted and sent out to 90 countries more than 85,000 volunteers. Many of them have come back to continue their education and are now professors, doctors, layers or social workers. A number have gone into international trade and banking and other business endeavors. About 500 are now on the staff of A.I.D. (Agency for International Development), the principal U.S. organization for foreign assistance to the Third World. Another 1,000 returned PCVs are employed in the State Department. The Reagan Administration's director for A.I.D. is Peter McPherson, himself a Peace Corps alumnus who served in Peru.

Many other Peace Corps people have come back from overseas assignments to join in the work of various religious and nonsectarian human-service groups at home and abroad. Africare, the first major black-run organization, through which private Americans may assist the peoples of Africa, was founded and is still led by C. Payne Lucas, one-time PC director for Niger and later for all of Africa. His deputy is Dr. Joseph Kennedy, former PC director for Sierra Leone and later the regional director for East Asia and the Pacific. A number of other service agencies have recruited staff members from the ranks of the Peace Corps.

Wherever former Peace Corps volunteers live and work, they are symbols of caring concern, inclined to be active in community service and, inevitably, bridges between their hometown neighbors and visitors and immigrants from abroad. Some outside observers—and many of the volunteers themselves—believe that one of the main achievements of the Peace Corps has been the expanded and enriched education, experience and global understanding it has provided for those who have had PC assignments abroad.

However true that may be, the chief purpose of the Peace Corps today, as in the past, is to help other people in the poorer, less developed countries help themselves.

Teaching English to high school students has been on of the most common Peace Corps assignments. It may not be the most glamorous way to help poor people, perhaps, but is is essential in this age in which English has become the most widely used language for communication around the globe—especially for those who are going to become leaders.

Today, as in years past, the Peace Corps receives repeated requests for volunteers who can teach sciences, mathematics, agriculture and industrial arts. There seem never to be enough young Americans available to fill these demands. This has encouraged the recruiting of men and women who are in mid-career or are retired. Often these older volunteers prove to be unusually successful, particularly those with skills in auto mechanics, electrical maintenance and building construction.

At the end of October 1981, the Peace Corps' oldest, longest serving volunteer retired at age 79, after 14 years of service in Gabon, Upper Volta and Sierra Leone. A skilled mechanic, who spent 40 years with a telephone company in Maine, Odilon ("Odie") Long started a new, exciting and immensely rewarding career after he had formally retired at age 65. The Corps could use a lot more Odie Longs.

Among other Peace Corps projects that are assisting grassroots economic development are windmills and mudbrick stoves. The shortage of energy is increasingly felt around the globe. For many poor rural people in Asia, Africa and Latin America, it is not a matter of escalating oil prices; they aren't buyers of petroleum products anyway. What bothers millions of people locked into traditional patterns of cooking and heating is the growing shortage of firewood. The Peace Corps has been trying to help with reforestation projects.

To further expand the varied activities of the Peace Corps, Director Ruppe has embarked on a program to attract more volunteers as well as more financial support from nongovernment sources.

Part of the task of broadening public awareness is simply making it known that the Peace Corps is still alive and working.

Back in the Nixon Administration days, somebody had the idea that the Peace Corps should be joined to domestic volunteer-service agencies such as Vista and other organizations. So a new umbrella organization, Action, was formed. People still argue over whether or not that was a sound step. In any case, during the Carter Administration, Congress moved to separate the Peace Corps from Action, making it again an independent agency. The reshuffle was completed at the end of President Reagan's first year in office, and the Peace Corps, once more, stands on its own. This change should help to make it more visible.

When the conservative government of Ronald Reagan arrived in Washington, there was a widespread belief that foreign aid would be drastically slashed, if not abolished. It didn't quite happen that way. Despite initial proposals by the Office of Management and Budget for cutting the A.I.D. budget in half and reducing the Peace Corps funding by about one-fourth, bipartisan support for maintaining a substantial assistance program won out. The Peace Corps allocation was held to $105 million. This represents, in actual value of the dollar, only about half the $114 million available to the Corps in 1966, when it had some 15,000 volunteers on duty in more than 70 countries. Today, there are roughly 5,000 PCVs in 60 Countries.

At the grassroots of American life, schoolchildren and ordinary citizens are becoming more deeply involved. The PTA in Rosendale, New York, raised money to help the community of Casa Blanca, Colombia, build a school. The Spanish Honor Society at T. C. Williams High School in Alexandria, Virginia, has been contributing to the support of a shelter for homeless boys on the outskirts of the city of Cali, Colombia. Such projects, part of the Peace Corps partnership program launched in 1964, have led to more learning on both sides about the "partner" community and have initiated numerous "pen pal" exchanges of letters and photographs. Other partnerships with other countries have been concerned with the construction and operation of clinics, nutrition centers, gardens and other community projects.

Loret Ruppe sees the entire Peace Corps operation as a prudent national investment of long-term benefit to the countries being helped, to the interests of the United States and to the peace of the world. She is thoroughly opposed, as is the president to whom she reports, to a hand-out approach to solving people's problems at home or abroad. But the Peace Corps, she points out, is one of those down-to-earth endeavors in which the emphasis is on helping people to help themselves—and it has a track record to prove that such an approach really works.

*With kind permission of the *Saturday Evening Post Society,* Copyright 1982

IVB Another Tribute To America's Peace Corps And Its Allies

by Vinson Brown

When America's Peace Corps truly increases the ability of the poor people of foreign lands to survive under difficulties, to be creative members of their society and particularly to improve the overall environment of their countries, it is doing a great service not only to each country served, and not only to the United States of America, but to the whole world. We can be proud of our Peace Corps and thankful to the wisdom of President Reagan in continuing it, but I think we need to realize that the very fact that the Peace Corps is doing a good job emphasizes our need to increase its effectiveness and its numbers and to spread its work more widely. Surely, just from a financial viewpoint alone, we should understand that the more helpful and creative we make the work of people in other countries the greater we open markets for the goods and services of America and the stronger we make these brother peoples in increasing freedom and democracy and so countering the forces of subversion and disruption that lead to tyranny!

There are more ways than one to increase the effectiveness and widespread influence of our Peace Corps. The first one we think of, of course, is increased appropriations from the American Congress, and we indeed need to ask for this, asking also, however, that the Peace Corps be sure to recruit and send abroad only people with sufficient know-how and training to be helpful in lifting the competence, effectiveness and well-being of people elsewhere.

Other good ways can be found to spread the Peace-Corps' influence. One is to get more and more of the super-national American corporations to realize that cooperation with the Peace Corps, even assisting them financially when a crisis shows the needs, will return far more to the company that helps than the money they cast upon the Peace Corps waters. This is because the

Peace Corps by developing self-reliance and know-how among the people it works with, especially the poor people, is both creating new customers for American companies, and also creating stable economic conditions for commerce and the production of both foods and goods. The benefits help prevent the negative conditions of civil conflict, crime and starvation so that more and more peaceful prosperity survives. Such companies as IBM, Bell Telephone and Xerox, have already pioneered in such efforts.

A third effort to spread the influence of America in the Peace Corps way is already under full steam from the Stephen Gaskin Community in Tennessee. Sometimes called the "Hippie Peace Corps" because it grew out of the Hippie movement towards communes in the 1960's, it yet gives something so fine and wonderful in its spreading of effective assistance to the growth of self-reliance among poor people in both America and abroad that it gives new light, strength and honor to the so-called "long-hairs" who take part in it. I have visited several so-called Hippie Communes in my time, and seen too much laziness and shiftlessness for good work or good management, but the Gaskin experiment is something else again of far different caliber. They have sent pioneer groups to such places as Guatemala, Bangledesh, Shri Lanka, and our own neglected and strip-mine destroyed parts of the Appalachian Mountains to train people in proper food production, renewal of wasted land, water purification, simple manufacturing and so on, that lift them from abject poverty towards self-reliance and true humanity. The Gaskin Community arose from poor people who practically elevated themselves by their boot-straps to create a healthy, happy, giving community, making the land better, the people better and moving on to help other parts of the earth.

More power to them, and to the Peace Corps and the newly unselfish giant corporations who are helping people everywhere end poverty and the blindness and ignorance that brings it! They have become towers of strength also in the struggle to bring peace and freedom to the whole world!

V The Healing Of The Nations*

by Donald Keys

For the first time in the earth's history humanity has an opportunity to become whole. The earth's shrinkage has amounted to a geographical implosion. To all reasonable intents and purposes, space and time are no more of any consequence in the relations of the human family.

This novel situation has, of course, sharply increased psychosocial tensions and frictions among the constituent nation-states and peoples of the world, which are not yet fitted into an organic, smoothly functioning pattern. Our sharply increased awareness of each other has also seemed to have caused a great increase in the problems facing humanity. I say, "seemed," since the problems, for the most part, have existed for some time, although their intensity has deepened greatly in recent years. We have become sensitized to problems of poverty, pollution, population, and peace on a global scale and have come to realize that solutions likewise must be planetary in scope if they are to be effective.

At the same time we are presented with opportunities that are even more significant than the problems. Buckminster Fuller states that "Humanity is going through its final examination to see if it can qualify for its universe function."[1] Whether it is humanity's final examination, it is without doubt its most important in all of human history. On the one hand, human survival is at stake. On the other, so is humanity's new role as conscious steward of evolution on this planet. Four billion years of earth's history have brought forth a species that is not only creative, self-actualizing, and capable of compassion and empathy, but also one that is globe-girdling and globe-dominant. The immediate corollary of course is *responsibility*. We have become responsible for the entire earthly domain. The open question before us is, Are we wise enough to execute that responsibility?

The execution of global responsibility depends upon the grounding and demonstration of appropriate human characteristics and values. These characteristics and values are no different from those required in good relations and effective collaboration among *individuals*. The same are now required from our largest human collectives--the nation-states.

What are some of these values and characteristics? There is nothing new about the homely values of goodwill, caring, and sharing; of making space in which others can grow and become; of helping to create environments that maximize the expression of human potential, alleviate suffering, allow and protect individuality, take responsibility for group good, limit and then transmute aggression, curb and moderate acquisitiveness and the violent and selfish pursuit of individual desires. These are values that have been found somehow not only to be socially necessary and desirable but also intrinsic in the evolving pattern of human growth as the capacity for decentralization and for identification with the hopes, needs, and wishes of others develops. They are necessary for the emergence of community. They are equally necessary for the emergence of *world* community. There must be some minimum threshold expression of these values on a global scale before humanity can integrate as the essential subjective unity it is and successfully manage planetary affairs.

The human family has produced some very valuable "letters of intent." Among the foremost might be mentioned the two United Nations human rights Covenants, regarded as binding treaty law, which establish planetary norms for the treatment of human beings. These are the *Covenant on Civil and Political Rights* and the *Covenant on Economic, Social and Cultural Rights*. The two Covenants are the expression in treaty form of the principles embodied in the *Universal Declaration of Human Rights*. They establish for the first time a planetary scale of values in these areas—an unparalleled achievement.

One must quickly add and acknowledge that these Covenants are often, if not usually, still honored in the breach; that even the United States has not yet ratified them; that codification is one thing and implementation a much more difficult step. For some countries and people particular human rights seem more significant and timely than others: the West is preoccupied with civil and political rights—rights to individual freedom and liberty. The south—the Third World, is much more concerned at present with rights to food, health care, education, clothing, and housing. These differences in current emphases must be respected and acknowledged while we insist that no human right is secure in the absence of the expression of others.

We also have before us on the international agenda the dim outlines of a value pattern for a global economic system. These have been set forth in the "Declaration on the New International Economic Order" and a "Charter of Economic Rights and Duties" adopted by the United Nations. These are certainly not perfect documents, and they brought sharp opposition from the biggest industrialized countries on a few points—for example, compensation for expropriated assets. Nevertheless, we are now on the way to defining and then to implementing the economic obligations of peoples for each other.

Ecological values have been institutionalized in a new UN Environment Program agency; those concerning health, education, and welfare, in the World Health Organization, UNESCO, and the UN Development Program.

There has thus been a successful transfer to the global level of the *principles* of commonly held human values. I say the "principles" since these agencies are still embryonic, weak, and poorly supported. However, the value transfer in itself is not only successful but immensely significant. It represents among other things a high degree of tacit international agreement on a definition of a human being—a surprising and unplanned development.

Set against the translation of humane values to the global level must be the pursuit by many nations of goals that are incompatible with world community well-being. We must also put on the deficit side of the equation collective aberrations and shortcomings of peoples-as-nations, aberrations that have strong analogues in individuals human behavior. Thus, for example, one of the main fuels of the suicidal nuclear arms race is erroneous threat perception — often based on "projection" of one's own notions or motivations. Nations tend to accept a "worst possible case" definition of the intentions of others. This leads to actions on their part, such as deploying a new and more destructive weapons system, which result in reciprocation and confirmation by the "enemy" state or states. Thus a self-fulfilling prophecy is produced, gravely *decreasing* the security of all concerned.

Another easily recognized psychological condition affecting the relations among states (as it also does among individuals) concerns the problem of communication. States, like individuals, tend to screen and to reject information at variance with that which they already have. They tend to accept information that reinforces their concepts of what is "true" and to reject contrary information as patently "untrue." This accounts to a large extent for the tardiness with which national attitudes and policies shift and for their almost continually lagging far behind newly perceived realities.

The question arises why the largest states often appear to have the most difficult time in perceiving and accommodating to change or in directing themselves to the perceived general interest of the world community. I have speculated that one factor might simply be *mass*. A large mass is less mobile—in this case, in opinion formation. It may also tend to be more ego-centered and self-involved. A large state traditionally cares little about the concerns and needs of the small. It may, once it does swing into action, act overwhelmingly and immovably on the basis of filtered information, half-digested "intelligence," and false assumptions.

In other respects, too, states resemble individual humans. No more than individuals are states unitary or wholly integrated. Just as the human is often a "divided house" of conflicting needs, aspirations, wishes, drives, and motivations, so is a nation. Some of these divided dominions can be identified as political parties, ethnic groups, and leadership groups from various economic strata, academia, large and powerful business and labor groups, and so on. These constitute, in a sense, some of the "subpersonalities" of nations. Often national objectives and policies necessarily reflect a "lowest common denominator" resulting from the goals and desires of these constituent dominions. Sometimes a forceful and well-motivated leader can challenge these groups to their best motivational potentialities.

* * *

Nations differ widely in their degree of integration and self-actualization. Some are much more value-oriented planetary citizens than others. The voting records of some nations at the

UN are consistently more community oriented, more expressive of responsibility and concern than others. A world community oriented scoring system that I have applied to voting at the UN General Assembly for a number of years consistently shows Australia, New Zealand, Yugoslavia, Singapore, Canada, the Nordic Group, Colombia, Venezuela, Nigeria, Ghana, and Sri Lanka among the "high" scores.[2]

It is interesting to observe that quite often countries maintain a forthright and community-minded international policy over a considerable time even when their internal situations contain strife and repression.

Perhaps the Scandinavian countries have an easier time than most in developing a constructive attitude toward world affairs. They have homogenous, relatively small populations whose basic needs are met and no serious internal problems. They have developed over time a level of social concern that has now extended as a natural development to the world community as well. Sweden and Norway, for example, are among the few countries to approach or reach the UN goal for official development aid.

National personalities are very recognizable if one has the advantage of an international or non-national perspective as Planetary Citizens should. There are new, fresh nations, with idealism and growing capacities—often represented by their finest people; there are old and cynical nations with great skills, often misapplied; there are late adolescents, like the U.S. and U.S.S.R., with very different and also very difficult (and not equal) motivational and adjustment problems.

Unfortunately, very little study has been given to the psychological characteristics and well-being of nations as such. Political figures are not given to what they would consider irrelevancies such as psychological speculations. Psychologists and psychiatrists have largely ignored the field partly out of fear of criticism by their colleagues. Some exceptions have been Bryant Wedge with his Institute for the Study of National Behavior; Professor Jerome Frank, formerly of Johns Hopkins; Professor Herbert Kelman of Harvard University; and Professor Charles Osgood, of the University of Illinois at Urbana. One very valuable study that should be mentioned, though published in 1964, is *Psychiatric Aspects of the Prevention of Nuclear War* formulated by the Committee on Social Issues of the Group for the Advancement of Psychiatry. It is unfortunate that there has been so little work done, since a clear understanding of the psychological states and stages of nations-as-entities can be crucial to understanding behavior and to initiating successful conflict-resolution measures. Serious personality, motivational, and perception differences between or among nations today can mean the expunging of the human race and the end of the human experiment on earth. I earnestly hope for the development of a new psychology of groups and collectives—most particularly of nation-states. As the concept of world community continues to develop, there is bound to be a growing recognition of the personality characteristics and problems of the primary actors in that community—the nation-states.

In regard to Western industrialized countries in particular, are there any indications of a hopeful nature suggesting a maturing of values and attitudes toward the rest of the community of which they are a part? There is one particular and quite new indication I should like to note. A trend away from consumerism, acquisition, and satisfaction of material fancies at all costs has become sufficiently apparent in the United State to have been the subject of an important study by Stanford Research Institute, a study directed to United States businessmen. Duane Elgin and Arnold Mitchell have termed the trend "Voluntary Simplicity."[3] They define the core values of voluntary simplicity as material simplicity: human scale; self-determination; ecological awareness; and personal growth. The authors find a significant proportion of the American population, as well as that of some other Western countries, is beginning to opt for voluntary simplicity rather than for what some feel is an endless and mindless pursuit of material ends.

A 1977 Harris Survey supports this contention, showing that "The American people have begun to show a deep skepticism about the nation's capacity for unlimited economic growth, and they are wary of the benefits that growth is supposed to bring. Significant majorities place a higher priority on improving human and social relationships and the quality of American life than on simply raising the standard of living....The majority views suggest...that a quiet revolution may be taking place in our national values and aspirations. Some of these attitudes reflect the energy crunch and the realization that the supply of raw materials is not boundless; others are a legacy of all those ideas that young people pressed for in the 1960's that have now begun to take root in the 1970's."[4]

The trend toward voluntary simplicity has many implications, especially in terms of maturity and in terms of a deeper emphasis on inner growth. Elgin found a close correlation between interest in the new psychologies and the practice of some form of meditation and an opting for voluntary simplicity. For our purposes such a trend within Western industrialized nations can become part of a significant accommodation between the wealthy, northern "have" states, and the "have not" southern countries. Such a value trend can smooth the way to new accommodations and understandings between these two groups. Thus we are privileged to witness important and significant value formations in process.

Nor is participation in the world community ultimately antithetical to, for example, United States traditions or concerns. The U.S. concern and penchant for effective management is quite naturally going to thrust it into the forefront of efforts at satisfactory and cooperative planetary management. A national acceptance of consensual and democratic decision making could allow the U.S. to take leadership in the introduction of these approaches in international forums.

Other international personalities are more intractible and difficult, holding per solutions for world problems in simplistic and outmoded ideological terms, while they hold their populations to regimes of sharply limited self-expression and, in a sense, to "enforced simplicity." However, if the world will persevere in a move toward cooperative and constructive directions, hold-out nations will have little choice but to fall back on "me-too-ism." This has, in fact, frequently occurred in UN forums, even where their initial opposition was adamant.

One must say, however, that in general world political leaders have tended to tramp on and exacerbate the raw nerves of the psychoses that nations suffer, an approach that has certainly not been found useful in treatment of individuals. They tend to respond in kind or to react in righteous indignation to the provocations of others rather than to seek the avenues that will allay suspicions, fear, and doubts and allow for the possibility of changes in attitude in morose nations-personalities. In this respect, we await our clinicians of nations. The United Nations itself is a fascinating and very promising psyshosocial arena. The major powers are, of course, a little disenchanted with the UN at present. This is primarily because the tight control that some of them used to exercise over the UN is no longer available to them now that the UN has become a universal instrument, and big and small nations must now compete on more equal terms for the exercise of nation-state policies. However, the intensity and continuous nature of communication at the UN provides multiple opportunities for dealing with the difficulties of interpersonal national relationships. To speak anecdotally, I have on more than one occasion been witness to skilled therapeutic handling of interpersonal problems and national policy questions by UN diplomats and secretariat people dealing with the suspicions, fears, and unreasonable doubts of diplomats from "closed-in" countries. I can say quite definitely that in many cases nations do tend to choose UN representatives who epitomize personally the condensed and specific psychological sets, difficulties, and cultural qualities of the countries they represent.

There are, of course, many levels to UN proceedings. There is the level of official government policy. There is a level of personal concerns and integrity that sometime enters in; and then, too, "national" and "personal" are not always the same. There are the unstated policies of the UN secretariat, which as a neuter civil servant, is expected to have none. In fact, however, the UN secretariat is a reservoir of both skills and vision and can often succeed in placing before nations the next steps needed for the common good of the world community.

There are further levels. There is a level born of the simple and concrete fact that elements from all parts of humanity are gathered there in one spot: a kind of sensitive switchboard to all of humanity—unique in history, unique in human experience. Approaching universality at present with 151 member states, the UN is one of the few locations on earth where some synthetic feeling of what humanity itself is can be grasped, felt, sensed, and experienced. I should like to assure you that quite apart from the conflicts and problems of nations, this is an unique and elevating experience. Willy-nilly deeper levels of experience and meaning emerge at the United Nations because of this fact. The unexpected impact is often remarked upon by short-term delegates or by visitors. Some major personal reformations in attitude have been accomplished by exposure to this unique total-human environment. As is so often the case, that which appears threatening is that which has not been experienced. When one comes to know first hand the aspirations and goals of others, the unknown loses its fear.

The UN provides a unique setting in which it is possible to step outside of any particular national framework and to view the world pattern with a new and detached perspective. The pragmatic, practical idealism of many members of delegations, of unsung civil servants of the secretariat, and of nongovernmental groups ("NGO's") close to the UN that have achieved this perspective constitutes a considerable "natural resource" upon which the world is only beginning to draw. There exists in and around the UN an informal but tangible network of such people that Planetary Citizens has dubbed a "humanity underground" concerned with the good of the community. They represent a group of "honest brokers" in the harmonization of competing or conflicting national goals and hold a clearer vision of world community needs than is available to persons bound by partisan national views.

The world public has yet to take the measure of the two secretaries-general, Dag Hammarskjold and U Thant, who personified this role and this view, and who, incidentally, were making concerted personal efforts at inner growth. U Thant was little known or appreciated by Westerners; his memoirs, *View from the UN* give some profound insights but are not as revealing of his intense inner life as was Dag Hammarskjold's spiritual diary *Markings*. Another reflective element has been added in recent years to the UN by Sri Chinnoy, who heads the UN Meditation Group, meeting twice weekly with the participation of secretariat members, delegates, and NGO's.

Thus the character of the UN may be quite different from newspaper accounts of the political confrontations, which remain, of course, a consistent feature of its proceedings. The UN is gaining in centrality and importance even while it is being decried, because it represents an historical imperative. A planetary center has become essential to the conduct of human affairs. In the UN a planetary core has been established, a point for focusing human synthesis. A new awareness is emerging in the world; and humanity itself, like Rip Van Winkle, is waking up, collectively to take a charge of its own affairs and of spaceship earth—and none too soon.

Mankind's consciousness now must stretch to a new level; our inclusiveness and identification must now include the entire human community—the fellow beings of our species—and that species must share an appreciation and reverence for all planetary life, if indeed it wishes to survive and persist on this planet.

The nations of mankind are approaching a new threshold beyond which they will be integrated as components of a new and self aware organism—global humanity. A virtual Copernican revolution in awareness confronts us, with the opportunity and the necessity for redefining our relations with each other within the species; for defining for the first time (because it is only now historically possible) the relation of the unit to the entirety; for redefining our relations with the planet, and in a sense, with the cosmos.

Such redefinitions, or their lack, are bound to have significant impact on the state of the mental health and well-being of nations and individuals. In the same sense that in the past, family, tribe, community, state, and nation have represented new aspects of ourselves that required new identifications, and incorporation into our mental and feeling world, now another step is required. The borders of the nation-state as the ultimate and final boundary of identification, of "self" and repository of loyalty are becoming less sharp now, and a sense of loss, frustration, and confusion will ensue for the person who does not take the step to the final planetary loyalty and identification. There can be no more an "out group" of the human family if survival is to be assured. We must enlarge our capacities for acceptance to include all peoples.

Thus it seems quite clear that human health and wholeness will depend henceforth, in addition to other factors, in crossing this new threshold to planetary awareness. We might even say that in a very real sense humankind, facing the *crisis* of becoming whole, faces the *possibility* of being healed.

*This essay is printed by permission of Branden Press, Inc., from the book, *Earth at Omega: Passage to Planetization* by Donald Keys.

[1] From comments received by Planetary Celebration, 24 October 1975, held in the state of New York.

[2] See Donald F. Keys, "Reports on the General Assembly of the United Nations," 1971-79. These reports have been published each year through the 1970s by Planetary Citizens.

[3] Duane Elgin and Arnold Mitchell, "Voluntary Simplicity," in *Guidelines* (Menlo Park, California: Stanford Research Institute, 1976), pp. 1-46.

[4] Data available from Harris Survey offices, New York, New York.

VI   The Whole-Earth Conspiracy

by Marilyn Ferguson

* * *

When you come to be sensibly touched, the scales will fall from your eyes; and by the penetrating eyes of love you will discern that which your other eyes will never see. —Francois Fenelon, 1651-1715

* * *

Victor Hugo prophesied that in the twentieth century war would die, frontier boundaries would die, dogma would die—and man would live. "He will possess something higher than these—a great country, the whole earth...and a great hope, the whole heaven."

* * *

Today there are millions of residents of that "great country, the whole earth." In their hearts and minds, war and boundaries and dogma have indeed already died. And they possess that large hope of which Hugo wrote.

They know each other as countrymen.

The Whole Earth is a borderless country, a paradigm of humanity with room enough for outsiders and traditionalists, for all our ways of human knowing, for all mysteries and all cultures. A family therapist says she urges her clients to discover not who is right or wrong but what they have as a family. We are beginning to make such an inventory of the Whole Earth. Every time one culture finds and appreciates the discovery of another, every time an individual relishes the talents or unique insights of another, every time we welcome the unexpected knowledge emerging from inside the self, we add to that inventory.

Rich as we are—together—we can do anything. We have it within our power to make peace within our torn selves and with each other, to heal our homeland, the Whole Earth.

We look around at all the reasons for saying No: the failed social schemes, the broken treaties, the lost chances. And yet there is the Yes, the same stubborn questing that brought us from cave to the moon in a flicker of cosmic time.

A fresh generation grows up into a larger paradigm; thus it has always been. In many science-fiction tales the adults are barred from the transformation experienced by a new generation. Their children grow irrevocably beyond them, into a larger reality.

Those of us born into the "broken-earth" paradigm have two choices: We can go to our graves with the old view, like the generations of die-hard scientists who insisted there were no such things as meteorites, or germs, or brainwaves, or vitamins—or, we can consign our old beliefs unsentimentally to the past and take up the truer, stronger perspective.

New Mind, New World

We can be our own children.

Not even the Renaissance has promised such a radical renewal; as we have seen, we are linked by our travels and technology, increasingly aware of each other, open to each other. In growing numbers we are finding how people can enrich and empower one another, we are more sensitive to our place in nature, we are learning how the brain transforms pain and conflict, and we have more respect for the wholeness of the self as the matrix of health. From science and from the spiritual experience of millions, we are discovering our capacity for endless awakenings in a universe of endless surprises.

At first glance, it may seem hopelessly utopian to imagine that the world can resolve its desperate problems. Each year fifteen million die in starvation and many more live in unrelenting hunger; every ninety seconds the nations of the world spend one million dollars on armaments; every peace is an uneasy peace; the planet has been plundered of many of its nonrenewable resources. Yet there have been remarkable advances as well. Just since the end of World War II, thirty-two countries with 40 percent of the world's population have overcome their problems of food scarcity; China is becoming essentially self-sufficient and has controlled its once-overwhelming population growth; there is a net gain in world literacy and in populist governments; concern for human rights has become a stubborn international issue.

We have had a profound paradigm shift about the Whole Earth.

We know it now as a jewel in space, a fragile water planet. And we have seen that it has no natural borders. It is not the globe of our school days with its many-colored nations.

We have discovered our interdependence in other ways, too. An insurrection or crop failure in a distant country can signal change in our daily lives. The old ways are untenable. All countries are economically and ecologically involved with each other, politically enmeshed. The old gods of isolationism and nationalism are tumbling, artifacts like the stone deities of Easter Island.

We are learning to approach problems differently, knowing that most of the world's crises grew out of the old paradigm—the forms, structures, and beliefs of an obsolete understanding of reality. Now we can seek answers outside the old frameworks, ask new questions, synthesize, and imagine. Science has given us insights into wholes and systems, stress and transformation. We are learning to read tendencies, to recognize the early signs of another, more promising, paradigm.

We create alternative scenarios of the future. We communicate about the failures of old systems, forcing new frameworks for problem-solving in every area. Sensitive to our ecological crisis, we are cooperating across oceans and borders. Awake and alarmed, we are looking to each other for answers.

And this may be the most important paradigm shift of all. *Individuals are learning to trust—and to communicate their change of mind.* Our most viable hope for a new world lies in asking whether a new world is possible. Our very questions, our anxiety, says that we care. If we care, we can infer that others care, too.

The greatest single obstacle to the resolution of great problems in the past was thinking they could not be solved—a conviction based on mutual distrust. Psychologists and sociologists have found that most of us are more highly motivated than we think each other to be! For instance, most Americans polled favor gun control but believe themselves in the minority. We are like David Riesman's college students who all said they did not believe advertising but thought everyone else did. Research has shown that most people believe themselves more high-minded than "most people." Others are presumed to be less open and concerned, less willing to sacrifice, more rigid. Here is the supreme irony: our misreading each other. Poet William Stafford wrote:

If you don't know the kind of person I am

and I don't know the kind of person you are
a pattern that others made may prevail in the world,
and following the wrong god home, we may miss our star.

Following the wrong god home, we have seen all of those we did not understand as alien, the enemy. Failing to comprehend each other's politics, cultures, and subcultures, which often are based on a different worldview, we questioned each other's motives ...denied each other's humanity. We have failed to see the obvious: "Most people," whatever their philosophy about how to get there, want a warless society in which we are all fed, productive, fulfilled.

If we see each other as obstacles to progress, our assumption is the first and greatest obstacle. Mistrust is a self-fulfilling prophecy. Our old-paradigm consciousness has guaranteed its own dark expectations; it is our collective negative self-image.

Now, as we are learning to communicate, as ever-increasing numbers of people are transforming their fear and finding their bonds with the rest of humanity, sensing our common yearnings, many of the planet's oldest, deepest problems show promise of breaking and yielding. The shift for which we have waited. a revolution of appropriate trust, is beginning. Instead of enemies, we are looking for allies everywhere.

Beneath the trappings of culture, anthropologists have said, lies a whole other world. When we understand it, our view of human nature will change radically. Now we confront an array of possible ways to be. The global village is a reality. We are joined by satellite, supersonic travel, four thousand international meetings each year, tens of thousands of multinational companies, international organizations and newsletters and journals, even an emergent pan-culture of music, movies, art, humor. Lewis Thomas observed:

> *Effortlessly, without giving it a moment's thought, we are*
> *capable of changing our language, music, manners, morals,*
> *entertainment, even the way we dress, all around the earth*
> *in a year's turning. We seem to do this by general agree-*
> *ment, without voting or even polling. We simply think our*
> *way along, pass information around, exchange codes disguised,*
> *as art, change our minds, transform ourselves.*
> *...Joined together, the great mass of human minds around*
> *the earth seems to behave like a coherent living system.*

The proliferating small groups and networks arising all over the world operate much like the coalitional networks in the human brain. Just as a few cells can set up a resonant effect in the brain, ordering the activity of the whole, these cooperating individuals can help create the coherence and order to crystallize a wider transformation.

Movements, networks, and publications are gathering people around the world in common cause, trafficking in transformative ideas, spreading messages of hope without the sanction of any government. Transformation has no country.

These self-organizing groups are very little like old political structures; they overlap, form coalitions, and support each other without generating a conventional power structure. There are environmental groups like Les Vertes in France and the Green Alliance in Great Britain, women's groups, peace groups, human rights groups, groups battling world hunger; thousands of centers and networks supporting "new consciousness," like Nexus in Stockholm; publications like Alterna in Denmark, New Humanities and New Life in Great Britain, linking many groups; symposia on consciousness in Finland, Brazil, South Africa, Iceland, Chile, Mexico, Rumania, Italy, Japan, the USSR.

From Power To Peace

We are changing because we must.

Historically, peace efforts have been aimed at ending or preventing wars. Just as we have defined health in negative terms, as the absence of disease, we have defined peace as nonconflict. But peace is more fundamental than that. Peace is a state of mind, not a state of the nation. Without personal transformation, the people of the world will be forever locked in conflict.

If we limit ourselves to the old-paradigm concept of averting war, we are trying to overpower darkness rather than switching on the light. If we reframe the problem—if we think of fostering community, health, innovation, self-discovery, purpose—we are already engaged in waging peace. In a rich, creative, meaningful environment there is no room for hostility.

War is unthinkable in a society of autonomous people who have discovered the connectedness of all humanity, who are unafraid of alien ideas and alien cultures, who know that all revolutions begin within and that you cannot impose your brand of enlightenment on anyone else.

The Vietnam War protests in the United States marked a critical turning point, a coming of age, as millions said, in effect, that you can't consign an autonomous people to a war they don't believe in. Other phenomena in recent years have been equally significant: fifteen thousand Germans marching in Cologne to oppose a new flicker of Nazism and to express their individual grief for the Holocaust. Catholics and Protestants risking their lives to embrace at a bridge in Northern Ireland, promising each other to work for peace. *"Peace Now,"* the Israeli movement launched by combat soldiers asking, "Give peace a chance."

After a recent congress in Vienna on the role of women in world peace, Patricia Mische wrote of *"the transformation already slowly in process among individuals and groups who, in a deep probing of their own humanness, are discovering the bonds they have with people everywhere."*

Can the arms race be reversed? *"A prior question,"* Mische said, *"would be, 'Can people—and nations—change their hearts and minds?'"* The Vienna participants seemed living testimony that the answer is Yes. At the close of the congress one participant asked, to tumultuous applause, that at future conferences speakers not be required to identify themselves by nationality. *"I am here as a planetary citizen,"* she said, *"and these problems belong to all of us."*

We need not wait for a leadership. We can begin to effect change at any point in a complex system: a human life, a family, a nation. One person can create a transformative environment for others through trust and friendship. A warm family or community can make a stranger feel at ease. A society can encourage growth and renewal in its members.

We can begin anywhere—everywhere. *"Let there be peace,"* says a bumper sticker, *"and let it begin with me."* Let there be health, learning, relationship, right uses of power, meaningful work....*Let there be transformation, and let it begin with me.*

All beginnings are invisible, an inward movement, a revolution in consciousness. Because human choice remains sacrosanct and mysterious, none of us can guarantee a transformation of society. Yet there is reason to trust the process. Transformation is powerful, rewarding, natural. It promises what most people want.

Perhaps that is why the transformed society exists already as a premonition in the minds of millions. It is the *"someday"* of our myths. The word *"new"* so freely used (new medicine, new politics, new spirituality) does not refer so much to something modern as to something imminent and long awaited.

The new world is the old—transformed.

Re-Choosing

In this century we have seen into the heart of the atom. We transformed it—and history—forever. But we have also seen into the heart of the heart. We know the necessary conditions for the changing of minds. Now that we see the deep pathology of our past, we can make new patterns, new paradigms. *"The sum of all our days is just our beginning...."*

Transformation is no longer lightning but electricity. We have captured a force more powerful than the atom, a worthy keeper of all our other powers.

We find our individual freedom, by choosing not a destination but a direction. You do not choose the transforma-tive journey because you know where it will take you but because it is the only journey that makes sense.

This is the homecoming so long envisioned. *"Condemn me and not the path,"* Tolstoi said. *"If I know the road home, and if I go along it drunk and staggering, does that prove that the road is not the right one? If I stagger and wander, come to my help.... You are also human beings, and you are also going home."*

The nations of the world, Tocqueville once said, are like travelers in a forest. Although each is unaware of the destination of the others, their paths lead inevitably toward meeting in the center of the forest. In this century of wars and planetary crisis, we have been lost in the forest of our darkest alienation. One by one the accustomed strategies of nation-states—isolation, fortification, retreat, domination—have been cut off.

We are pressed ever more deeply into the forest, toward an escape more radical than any we had imagined: freedom with—not from—each other. After a history of separation and mistrust, we converge on the clearing.

Our metaphors of transcendence have spoken of us more truly than our wars: the clearing, the end of winter, the watering of deserts, the healing of wounds, light after darkness—not an end to troubles but an end to defeat.

Over the centuries those who envisioned a transformed society knew that relatively few shared their vision. Like Moses, they felt the breezes from a homeland they could see in the distance but not inhabit. Yet they urged others on to the possible future. Their dreams are our rich, unrealized history, the legacy that has always existed alongside our wars and folly.

In a wider state of consciousness one can sometimes vividly re-experience a past trauma and, in retrospect and with imagination, respond to it differently. By thus touching the source of old fears, we can exorcise them. We are not haunted so much by events as by our beliefs about them, the crippling self-image we take with us. We can transform the present and future by reawakening the powerful past, with its recurrent message of defeat. We can face the crossroads again. We can re-choose.

In a similar spirit, we can respond differently to the tragedies of modern history. Our past is not our potential. In any hour, with all the stubborn teachers and healers of history who called us to our best selves, we can liberate the future. One by one, we can re-choose—to awaken. To leave the prison of our conditioning, to love, to turn homeward. To conspire with and for each other.

Awakening brings its own assignments, unique to each of us, chosen by each of us. Whatever you may think about yourself, and however long you may have thought it, you are not just you. You are a seed, a silent promise. You are the conspiracy for a whole earth!

* * *

*A part of the last chapter of *The Aquarium Conspiracy* by Marilyn Ferguson, (J. P. Tarcher Inc.) 1981, by permission of Marilyn Ferguson.

VII PEACE AS A PARADIGM SHIFT*

by Dr. Michael N. Nagler

Science advances through a succession of "paradigms," or frames of reference, which are often mutually irreconcilable, according to Thomas S. Khun's familiar description. The term "paradigm," widely adopted in the social sciences, has become almost common parlance.

In the process, however, it has lost some of its meaning. People now speak of paradigms wherever two or more concepts show any semblance of systematic coherence. They also speak as if a babble of different paradigms—"Marxist, realist traditionalist, peace research, feminist, and behavioralist," to quote one recent catalogue—could exist side by side. Everyone has the right to use the term as he or she wishes, but this is not the sense in which Kuhn intended it.

Kuhn was concerned to show that even in science, where the raw data of the scientist's observation can be limited and controlled, they would be unmanageably complex without some previously agreed upon frame of reference. He showed that such a frame of reference involves preset categories which soon become deeply rooted in the perceptual and thinking process, and that, until "paradigm breakdown" and "paradigm shift" occur, it is widely if not universally shared throughout the community of discourse. One can be a Marxist and a feminist; one cannot believe in a Ptolemaic and Copernican universe.

This is not to say that people do not use preset categories in life, as they do in sciences; on the contrary. As William James pointed out, without selective perception to screen out the majority of our sense data and our own thoughts, life, even more than science, would be past coping with. As Hazlitt put it, "Without the aid of prejudice and custom I should not be able to make my way across the room."

Yet in life, even more than in science, paradigms can be disastrous failures. Or to speak historically, paradigms that have provided a useful system of selective perception, evaluation and decision for a time can become worse than useless encumbrances and require wholesale replacement for society to advance.

That is precisely the position we have now reached with the prevailing attitudes about militarism and war. Many peace researchers today would agree that the achievement of stable peace conditions in the world will require a paradigm shift. They may not all realize, however, that the shift required will not be that spoken of loosely by the social scientists, but the much deeper and broadly accepted change of vision described by Kuhn.

What is needed is not just a change of opinion, like the oscillations in public legitimacy in the United States accorded to the Vietnam War, but a permanent shift in how we view the world: how we gauge hostility, what we think of to do about it—almost a shift in what we perceive as real. Aristotle actually "saw" constrained fall in a stone swinging back and forth on the end of a string, Galileo saw the glimmerings of momentum in exactly the same phenomenon. As long as people feel comfortable when they make threats to other nations of people whom they regard as enemies and fail to perceive that those "enemies" will respond by making counterthreats (just as they themselves do), it will not be possible to abolish war.

It is true that individual wars can be aborted by better diplomacy. It is also true that the tendency of nations to get into dangerous confrontations can be mitigated by the institution of more rational political and social systems within them. But if we want to eliminate the root cause of war—and in this nuclear era we cannot dare to stop short of this, if we want to live in the security of knowing that the exploitive economies, which put nations at one another's throats have been abandoned for good and that nations no longer act with the dangerous irrationality of adolescents in the schoolyard (as Norman Cousins once said), then we need to go after the causes of war which lie "in the minds of men."

Emerson quite correctly said, "It was a thought that built this whole portentous war establishment, and a thought shall melt it away." But what he meant by "thought" is poetic shorthand for a whole way of thinking. If a true paradigm shift in science is a rare event which occurs only after a lapse of centuries, the shift we are speaking of is even rarer. It is a reorientation of the attitude of masses of human beings not only to a particular war, not only to war in general, but to our relationships with one another. It is a step forward not only in history but in biological evolution.

The questions that anyone concerned with peace today must ask, therefore, are two:

Are the times right for a perceptual revolution of this magnitude?

If so, what can I do to facilitate it?

We have an answer to the first question, as simple as it is remarkable, from Kenneth Boulding, past president of the American Association for the Advancement of Science. In his latest book, *Stable Peace* (1978), Boulding has formulated what he sees as the extraordinary watershed in which mankind now finds itself with regard to the most important question for continued survival: "War is no longer legitimate." If this is correct, we have reached what Kuhn would call an incipient paradigm breakdown which has not yet been carried through, for want of a paradigm shift.

And of course it is correct. Almost daily more disturbing anomalies confront those who still believe that political power grows out of the barrel of a gun—or a nuclear silo: The militarily strongest nation in the world is unable to control events in a tiny Southeast Asian country; to react effectively when its diplomatic staff is taken hostage in the Middle East; to preserve its economy; to maintain a foreign policy concensus at home, or the ability of its citizens to walk down the street in safety. The number two military power is in a similar predicament. Both add to their own and one another's insecurity with each new generation of weapons they produce to gain security.

To the majority, who are good Ptolemaeans, these problems, all of which are directly or indirectly produced by our commitment to military power, are still what Kuhn calls "puzzles" in a system which remains generally sound. But to a growing number of more thoughtful "Copernicans," from every walk of life, these problems are not puzzles but genuine "counterinstances" showing that the entire paradigm in which they are sustained is wrong.

Can we get people to abandon the old paradigm? Only if and when we can get them to see a new one. As Kuhn observes, "once it has achieved the status of a paradigm, a scientist theory is declared invalid only if an alternative candidate is available to take its place.... The decision to reject one paradigm is always simultaneously the decision to accept another." There can be no question of perception, evaluation and decision *without* a paradigm. That may be possible for the mystic, but it cannot be the ordinary process of human decision-making in science, and still less in politics.

Significant numbers of people will never stop making the decisions that lead inevitably to war, even if the resulting wars destroy everything they live for, until and unless they come to trust, understand and learn the use of an entirely new system of decisions that leads to peace. Fortunately, such a system is already known. These words of Albert Szent-Gyeorgyi point to it very clearly:

"Between the two world wars, at the heyday of Colonialism, force reigned supreme. It had a suggestive power, and it was natural for the weaker to lie down before the stronger.

"Then came Ghandi, chasing out of his country, almost single-handed, the greatest military power on earth. he taught the world that there are higher things than force, higher even than life itself; he proved that force had lost its suggestive power."

Any successful use of non-violence—the liberation of India from British rule is a conspicuous example—provides not only an arresting counterinstance to the old paradigm of injurious force but a clear indication of the new paradigm. It is based on an entirely different set of assumptions and a different system of human relationships. The term "nonviolence," like that of "paradigm," has been weakened in the social sciences and in its rare appearances in common parlance. But when truly understood it provides an entirely new conceptual system, and when correctly applied it provides mankind, in Gahndi's words, with "the greatest force he has ever been endowed with."

Life theories, of course, are even harder to change than scientific theories. But the method history shows us is the same: First a few daring geniuses discern the new paradigm—a Copernicus, a Galileo, an Einstein, or in our case a Gahndi. Then certain opinion leaders take it up and demonstrate its power. In course of time it becomes the established frame of reference. That is why Einstein reckoned that if only 5 percent of the people would work actively on peace it would be achieved. Peace is not only inherently more desirable but practically more workalbe than war, and as with any such change, when opinion leaders begin to use the new paradigm what was at first the "lunatic fringe" can become insensibly, but rapidly enough, the carpet on which the majority takes its stand.

Our second question—what can I do—has therefore almost answered itself. Whatever we can do to increase the visibility of this new paradigm would be far and away the most effective contribution we can make to the establishment of a lasting peace. There are many ways to approach this adventure, but it seems to me that for all of us who are members of the intellectual community these ways would entail our learning the history of nonviolence, understanding the theory behind it, and—most importantly—learning to practice it. What the *Report from Iron Mountain* (by Leoanard C. Lewin, Dell) had to say in 1967, that "up to now, no one had taken more than a timid glance over the brink of peace," is still far too true.

At present, as we know to our cost, certain "buzz words" like "strength," "preparedness" and above all "security," because they are thin disguises for *military* strength, and *military* security, play a major role in systematically misleading the policy decisions of people from the lowest to the highest political echelon. The most effective way to attack that kind of outmoded thinking is to point out, and where possible demonstrate, that there is a greater strength in cooperation and "mutual aid" than in belligerency; that any security worthy of the name can only come from not having enemies, not from threatening those we perceive as enemies. We have to know about the successful uses of nonthreatening protective mechanism like nonviolent civil defense, and about other aspects of the nonviolent armamentarium to carry this point.

It is not uncommon to see a newspaper headline like "What U.S. Could Do to Iran" (meaning of course, what harm we could do to Iran). These questions are in the genre, "when did you last beat your wife?" They preclude any consideration of the one question which is in fact most important: *Should* we harm them?" The most effective way to open people's eyes to that neglected question is not to point out how we provoked the Iranians by harming them in the first place. (It may be true but it does not seem to be effective.) Rather, it is to demonstrate how cooperative and conciliatory behavior would be a more efficient way to deal with them than combative aggression.

Without a definite shift in our educational perspective we can hardly hope to effect a permanent shift in our world view. The things that unite the various people of the globe would have to be made more interesting than the present intellectual fascination with differences. Such a shift would prepare the ground for this opening of eye. We would have to know not only how the principle of peace is being violated all over the world, but precisely what it would take to make peace more stable, which as far as I can see can only be thoroughgoing nonviolence.

At the basis of the old, increasingly vulnerable but still very dangerous paradigm of force and violence there is the central assumption that people are separate, pretty much as they appear to the senses. We will never securely abolish war without challenging this basic assumption; and the new paradigm does challenge it. Nonviolence is based on the hypothesis that all life is one.

Just as Einstein opened the modern era in physics by challenging the accepted axiom that time and space are absolute coordinates, so he and others now challenge us with the even more portentous hypothesis that men and women are not separate from one another and the rest of the environment. The day may be dawning—we should see to it that it does dawn—when these words of Einstein are as much used as his famous formula expressing the interconvertibility of matter and energy:

"A human being is part of the whole, called by us the 'universe,' a part limited in time and space. He experiences himself, his thoughts and feelings, as something separate from the rest — a kind of optical delusion of his consciousness. This delusion is a kind of prison for us, restricting us to our personal desires and to affection for a few persons nearest to us. Our task must be to free ourselves from this prison by widening our circle of compassion to embrace all living creatures and the whole nature in its beauty."

When Gahndi called nonviolence a science, as he often did, and referred to his own life as a series of experiments with truth he was not being metaphorical. Nonviolence is certainly science. It can be learned, and taught. It has a central hypothesis, as we have seen, from which a system of theoretical and practical constructs about the nature of reality have begun to be developed and tested. Its laboratory is the whole of life, and the scientists competent fo explore it are, literally, all of us.

During the recent debates on the connection of the University of California with the national nuclear weapons laboratories a distinguished physicist explained to us that he was voting to retain that connection because. "I guess I'm older than most of you, and I can remember what happened to France in 1939." If my colleague could remember what happened to France in 1939, why could he not remember what happened to India on August 15, 1947, when the last British detachments, cheered by vast crowds of friendly Indians, sailed willingly for home?

It is not lack of experience but lack of a sufficient paradigm in which to interpret that experience that caused his selective perception, and the decision he based on it. Our job is not one of dissuasion but of education. Let each person truly know what happens to a country that can perceive only military force and becomes dependent on military defense, and what happens when a country learns to wield "the greatest force that mankind has been endowed with." I have enough confidence in human nature to know what his or her choice would be.

VIII Cease This Madness

by George F. Kennan*

In the eyes of the former ambassador to Moscow, the two superpowers have reached a moment of unparalleled tension and danger. Can they turn away from the irrationalities of the arms race?

* * *

When I glance back over the past fifty years, it seems evident that the East-West relationship has been burdened by certain unique factors that lie in the very nature of the resepctive societies. When it comes to describing these factors, permit me—so far as the Western side is concerned—to confine myself to my own society.

I have no doubt that there are a number of habits, customs, and uniformities of behavior, all deeply ingrained in the American tradition, that complicate for others the conduct of relations with the American government. There is, for example, the extensive fragmentation of authority throughout our government—a fragmentation that often makes it hard for a foreign representative to know who speaks for the American government as a whole. There is the absence of any collective Cabinet responsibility, or indeed of any system of mutual responsibility between the executive and legislative branches of government. There are the large powers exercised, even in matters that affect foreign relations, by state, local, or private authorities with which the foreign representative cannot normally deal. There is the susceptibility of the political establishment to the emotions and vagaries of public opinion, particularly in this day of confusing interaction between the public and the various commercialized mass media. There is the inordinate influence exercised over American foreign policy by individual lobbies and other organized minorities. And there is the extraordinary difficulty a democratic society experiences in taking a balanced view of any other country that has acquired the image of a military and political enemy—the tendency, that is, to dehumanize that image, to oversimplify it, to ignore its complexities. Democratic societies do very poorly in coping, philosophically, with the phenomenon of serious challenge and hostility to their values.

In the light of these conditions, I can well understand that dealing with our government can be a frustrating experience at times for any foreign representative. I regret these circumstances, as do some other Americans. They constitute one of the reasons I personally advocate a more modest, less ambitious American foreign policy than do many of my compatriots.

But these conditions flow from the very nature of our society, and they are not likely to be significantly changed at any early date.

When we look at the Soviet regime, we also encounter a series of customs and habits, equally deeply rooted in history and weighing heavily on the external relationships of that regime. These, strangely enough, seem to have been inherited much less from the models of the recent Petersburg epoch than from those of the earlier Grand Duchy of Muscovy. And they have found a remarkable reinforcement in some of the established traditions of Leninist Marxism itself: in its high sense of orthodoxy, its intolerance for contrary opinion, its tendency to identify ideological dissent with moral perversity, its ingrained distrust of the heretical outsider.

One example is the extraordinary passion for secrecy in all governmental affairs—a passion that prevents the Soviet authorities from revealing to outsiders even those aspects of their own motivation that, if revealed, would be reassuring to others. Excessive secrecy tends, after all, to invite excessive curiosity, and thus serves to provoke the very impulses against which it professes to guard.

Along with this passion for secrecy goes a certain conspiratorial style and tradition of decision-making, particularly within the Party—a practice that may have its internal uses but often inspires distrust. And there is the extraordinary espionomania that appears to pervade so much of Soviet thinking. Espionage is a minor nuisance, I suppose, to most governments. But nowhere, unless it be in Albania, is the preoccupation with it so intense as it appears to be in the Soviet Union. This is surprising, for one would expect to encounter it, if anywhere, in a weak and precariously situated state, not in one of the world's greatest and most secure military powers.

The foreigner who has to deal with the Soviet government often has the impression of being confronted, in rapid succession, with two quite disparate, and not easily reconcilable, Soviet personalities: one, a correct and reasonably friendly personality, which would like to see the relationship assume a normal, relaxed, and agreeable form; the other, a personality marked by a suspiciousness so dark and morbid, so sinister in its implications, as to constitute in itself a form of hostility. I sometimes wonder whether the Soviet leaders ever realize how much they damage their own interests by their cultivation of it.

Finally, there is the habit of polemic exaggeration and distortion, carried often to the point of denial of the obvious and solemn assertion of the absurd—a habit that has offended and antagonized a host of foreigners, and to which even some of the old-timers find it hard to accustom themselves.

These, then, are what I might call the permanent complications of the East-West relationship. There have been others, less permanent but even more serious.

The first, and the one that marked the relationship throughout much of the 1920s and 1930s, was the world-revolutionary commitment of the early Leninist regime, with its accompanying expression in rhetoric and activity. It is true that the period of the intensive pursuit of world revolution was brief. As early as 1921, aims of this nature were already ceasing to enjoy the highest priority in the policies of the Kremlin. Their place was being taken by concern with the preservation of the regime and the agricultural and industrial development of the country. But world-revolutionary rhetoric remained substantially unchanged throughout the twenties and much of the thirties; and Moscow continued to maintain in the various Western countries small factions of local Communist followers over whom it exerted the strictest discipline, whom it endeavored to use as instruments for the pursuit of its policies, and whose unquestioning loyalty it demanded even when this conflicted with loyalty to their own governments. So unusual were these practices, and so disturbing to Western governments and publics, that they formed the main cause for the high degree of tension between Russia and the West.

With the triumph of Hitler in Germany, however, an important change occurred. Beginning about 1935, the menace of Hitler began to loom larger in Western eyes than did the ideological differences with Soviet communism or the resentment of world-revolutionary activities. The result was that the Soviet Union came to be viewed in the West no longer primarily from the standpoint of its hostility to Western capitalism but rather from the standpoint of its relationship to Nazi Germany.

And this had several confusing consequences. For one thing, it tended to obscure from the attention of the Western public the full savagery of the Stalinist purges of the late 1930s. but then, after 1941 the common association of the Western powers with the Soviet Union in the war against Germany gave rise to senti-mental enthusiasms in the West and to unreal hopes of a happy and constructive postwar collaboration with Soviet Russia. It was this factor, as the war came to an end, that brought the various Western statesmen to accept without serious remonstrance not only the recovery by the Soviet Union of those border areas of the former Russian empire that had been lost at the time of the Revolution but also the establishment of a virtual Soviet military-political hegemony over the remainder of the eastern half of the European continent; in other words, a geopolitical change of historic dimensions, bound to complicate the restoration, in the postwar years, of anything resembling a really stable balance of power.

It was not surprising that when the war came to an end, and people in the West turned to the construction of a new world order, a reaction set in. There was a sudden realization that the destruction of Germany's armed power and the effective cession to the Soviet Union of a vast area of military deployment in the very heart of the continent had left Western Europe highly vulnerable to a Soviet military attack, or at least to heavy military-political pressure from the Soviet side. Added to this was the growing realization that with the establishment of Communist regimes, subservient to Moscow, in the various Eastern European countries, the relations of those countries with the West had become subject to the same limiting factors that already operated in relations with the soviet Union. Then came the Korean War—a conflict in which, though soviet forces were not actually involved, people in the West soon came to see a further manifestation of Soviet aggressiveness. And it was just at this time that the nuclear weapon began to cast its baleful shadow over the entire world, stirring up the fear, confusion, and defensive panic that were bound to surround a weapon of such apocalyptic—indeed, suicidal—implications.

The death of Stalin, the establishment of the dominant position of Khrushchev, and the accompanying relaxations in Soviet policy gave rise to new hopes for the peaceful resolution of East-West differences. Although Khrushchev was crude, he wanted no war; and he believed in human communication. But he overplayed his hand. And such favorable prospects as his influence presented went largely without response in the West. The compulsions of military competition and military thinking were already too powerful.

For, during this entire period, Soviet leaders persisted in the traditional Russian tendency to go too far in the cultivation of military strength, particularly conventional strength. They continued to maintain along their western borders, as their czarist predecessors had done before them, forces numerically greater than anyone else could see the need for. And the situation was not made better by the tendency of Western strategists and military leaders to exaggerate the strength of these forces, with a view to wheedling larger military appropriations out of their own reluctant parliaments, or by the tendency of the Western media to dramatize these exaggerations as a means of capturing public attention.

The Americans, meanwhile, unable to accommodate to the recognition that the long-range nuclear missile had rendered their country no longer defensible, threw themselves headlong ino the nuclear arms race, followed at every turn by the Russians. In the U-2 episode and the Cuban missile crisis, the two great nuclear powers traded fateful mistakes, further confirming each other's conviction that armed force, and armed force alone, would eventually determine the outcome of their differences. Out of all these ingredients was brewed the immensely disturbing and tragic situation in which we find ourselves today: anxious competition in the development of new armaments; blind dehumanization of the prospective adversary; systematic distortion of that adversary's motivation and intentions; steady displacement of political considerations by military ones in the calculations of statesmanship; in short, a dreadful militarization of the entire East-West relationship.

This moral and political cul-de-sac represents a basic change, as compared with the first two decades of Soviet power, in the source of East-West tensions. It is not the capacity of the Kremlin for promoting social revolution in other countries that is feared and resented. Rather, the soviet Union is seen primarily as an aggressive military menace.

But there is no rational reason for the militarization of the Cold War. Neither side wants a third world war. Neither side sees in such a war a promising means of advancing its interests. The West has no intention of attacking the Soviet Union. The Soviet leadership, I am satisfied, has no intention of attacking Western Europe. The interests of the two sides conflict, to be sure, at a number of points. Experience has proven, most unfortunately, that in smaller and more remote conflicts, where the stakes are less than total, armed force on a limited scale might still continue to play a certain role, whether we like it or not. The United States has used its armed forces in this manner three times since World War II: in Lebanon, in the Dominican Republic, and in Vietnam. The Soviet Union now does likewise in Afghanistan. I am not entertaining, by these remarks, the chimera of a total world disarmament. But for the maintenance of armed forces on a scale that envisage the total destruction of an entire people there is no rational justification. Such a practice can flow only from fear, and irrational fear at that. It can reflect no positive aspirations, and it is dangerous.

No one will understand the danger we are all in today unless he recognizes that governments in this modern world have not yet learned how to create and cultivate great military establishments, particularly those that include the weapons of mass destruction, without becoming the servants rather than the masters of what they have created. Modern history offers no example of the cultivation by rival powers of armed force on a huge scale that did not in the end lead to an outbreak of hostilities. And there is no reason to believe that we are greater, or wiser, than our ancestors. It would take a very strong voice, indeed a powerful chorus of voices, from the outside, to say to the decision-makers of the two superpowers what should be said to them:

"For the love of God, of your children, and of the civilization to which you belong, cease this madness. You have a duty not just to the generation of the present; you have a duty to civilization's past, which you threaten to render meaningless, and to its future, which you threaten to render nonexistent. You are mortal men. You are capable of error. You have no right to hold in your hands—there is no one wise enough and strong enough to hold in his hands—destructive powers sufficient to put an end to civilized life on a great portion of our planet. No one should wish to hold such powers. Thrust them from you. The risks you might thereby assume are not greater—could not be greater—than those which you are now incurring for us all."

But where is the voice powerful enough to say it?

There is a very special tragedy in this weapons race. It is tragic because it creates the illusion of a total conflict of interest between the two societies. It tends to conceal the fact that both of these societies are today confronted with internal problems never envisaged in the ideologies that originally divided them. In part, I am referring to environmental problems: the question whether great industrial societies can learn to exist without polluting, exhausting, and thus destroying the natural resources essential to their very existence. These are not only problems common to the two ideological worlds; they are ones the solution of which requires each other's collaboration, not each other's enmity.

But there are deeper problems—social, and even moral and spiritual—that increasingly affect all the highly industrialized, urbanized, and technologically advanced societies. What is involved here is essentially the question of how life is to be given an adequate meaning, how the quality of life and experience is to be assured for the individual citizen in the highly artificial and overcomplicated social enviroment that modern technology has created. Neither we in the West nor they in the East are doing well in the solution of these problems. We are both failing—each in our own way. If one wants an example of this, one has to look only at our respective failures in our approach to teenage youth. The Russians demoralize their young people by giving them too little freedom. We demoralize ours by giving them too much. Neither system finds itself able to provide them with the leadership and inspiration and guidance needed to realize their potential as individuals and to meet the responsibilites the Future is inevitably going to place upon them.

And this is only one point at which we are failing. Neither here nor there is the direction of society really under control. We are all being swept along, in our fatuous pride, by currents we do not understand and over which we have no command. And we will not protect ourselves from the resulting dangers by continuing to pour great portions of our substance, year after year, into the instruments of military destruction. On the contrary, we will only be depriving ourselves, by this prodigality, of the resources essential for any hopeful attack on these profound emerging problems.

The present moment is in many respects a crucial one. Not for thirty years has political tension reached so dangerous a point as it has attained today. Not in all this time has there been so high a degree of misunderstanding, of suspicion, of bewilderment, and of sheer military fear.

The United States and possibly the Soviet Union will see extensive changes in in governmental leadership this year. Will the new leaders be able to reverse these trends?

Two things, as I see it, would be necessry to make possible this transition.

First, statesmen on both sides should take their military establishments in hand and insist that these become the servants, not the masters and determinants, of political action. Both sides must learn to accept the fact that only in the reduction, not in the multiplication, of existing monstrous arsenals can the true security of any nation be found.

But beyond this, we must learn to recognize the gravity of the social, environmental, and even spiritual problems that assail us all in this unreal world of the machine, the television screen, and the computer. We and our Marxist friends must work together in finding hopeful responses to these insidious and ultimately highly dangerous problems.

IX   Compassion, Science And World Peace

by Vinson Brown

Nikita Kruschev, former Premier of Russia, was visiting President Eisenhower at Camp David, Maryland, in 1958, when he asked the President how he got along with his War Department. Ike replied: "My military come to me and say, 'Mr. President, we need such and such a sum for such and such a program.' I say, 'Sorry, we don't have the funds.' They say, 'We have reliable information that the Soviet Union has already allocated funds for their own such program.' —So I give in. That's how they wring money out of me! Now tell me, how is it with you?"

"It's just the same!" Kruschev exclaimed. "We really should come to some sort of agreement in order to stop this fruitless and wasteful rivalry!"[1]

Sensible words indeed! But unfortunately, a real chance to establish world peace was lost because soon the old fears, prejudices and misunderstandings between the two nations were fanned up again.

It is this jumping from friendliness to suspicion and back again between Russia and America, which has happened frequently, that is one of the major reasons why it is so difficult to move our world towards lasting peace. Yet there is no more important step for the human race to take in all its history than an advance into permanent peaceful relations between nations. The alternative today is a war with weapons so terrible that vast numbers of life on this planet could be destroyed.

I believe a combination of compassion and scientific method can lead us out of the swamp of friction and misunderstanding we are now in, and help us achieve world peace. Compassion is actually a major phase of religion, so that essentially what I am claiming is needed is a partnership between science and enlightened religion. We must be compassionate towards others if we desire compassion for ourselves. Compassion is now desperately needed for all the children and all the other life of this earth, for we are in grave danger of losing much of those precious lives in a hydrogen bomb war. How can compassion be joined with science to prevent this most terrible of all catastrophes? Let us see first how science alone could have prevented disasters this country has already had.

To understand the scientific method is first to understand what it is not, and to learn how it can prevent disastrous errors in judgment. There were three fairly recent great tragedies in American history that I am sure could have been prevented had the scientific method been used. The first was the incredible calamity at Pearl Harbor on December 7, 1941, when much of the United States fleet was destroyed by Japanese bombers. There was plenty of warning that this might happen. Why then did the commanding naval and army officers at Pearl Harbor not take proper precautions? It was mainly because they considered this great Hawaiian Base an impregnable fortress and also misjudged the Japanese, believing them an inferior people. They became trapped in their own narrow logic, reinforced each other's complacency, and made no attempt to investigate carefully other alternatives, as is basic to the scientific method.

Exactly the same kind of illogical blindness of a similar group of supposedly intelligent leaders happened in November 1950 when General MacArthur was allowed by military higher-ups and President Truman to plunge his army recklessly into North Korea and try to conquer all at one blow. But China's immense army soon thrust his forces back to South Korea.

A third disaster, based on similar faulty reasoning, happened with the Bay of Pigs Invasion of Cuba, instigated by the Central Intelligence Agency on April 17, 1961, and approved by President Kennedy.

Fortunately, after this fiasco, President Kennedy was a big enough man to ask two important questions. The first was: "How could we have been so stupid?" which led him and his advisers to carefully analyze the mistakes all had made. Second, he wanted to know: "How can we prevent this from happening again in the next crisis?"

He realized that something like the scientific method of examining all alternatives and questions thoroughly and with an equally open mind was necessary. In October, 1962, a new and great emergency was caused by the Soviet Union answering Cuba's call for help against another possible U.S. invasion be sending Russian missiles and missile launchers to the island. When President Kennedy realized what was happening, he called up, not only his former advisers, but also experts from outside, including scientists, and people knowledgeable of Russia, to consider every alternative of how to answer this challenge.

The military officers, whose advice was also asked, opted for either an invasion of Cuba or a heavy bombing of the new missile bases. Kennedy, the scientists and other advisers, felt this could bring on full-scale war. Using the scientific method, they carefully examined all alternatives with equally open minds, presented every possible argument for each, listened carefully to the experts on Russia so they could understand the Russian leaders, and decided finally on a very careful and low-key blockade of the Cuban coast to keep out the missiles, combined with courteous words to the Russians that it would be better for everybody concerned if the missiles were withdrawn. The Russians agreed, provided the U.S. promised not to invade Cuba. This was done and World War III was prevented!

This result recalls the famous fable of Aesop, in which the Wind challenged the Sun to see who could force a man to take off his cloak the fastest. The Sun agreed and the Wind tried first. He blew as hard and coldly as he could, but the more he blew the more tightly the man held onto his cloak. Finally the Wind gave up, but the Sun had only to turn on his warm rays nd very soon the cloak came off!

Following the wisdom of the Sun and his warmth, and developing a well-balanced team of scientists and other experts, much as President Kennedy formed at the time of the Cuban Missile Crisis, we can call on the other nations of the world, and particularly Russia, to join with us, not in a competition or a big argument over peace, but a solid and a mature approach in which all are asked to collaborate intelligently and cooperatively in producing the finest and most stable relations between nations possible with justice and safety from aggression for all. And the guiding light which should drive all who partake in this mightiest and most heroic effort of all history to rise to the noblest heights of selfless devotion for all humankind is the compassion all who partake must have in their hearts for the priceless lives, the happiness and the future of the millions, no billions, of innocent children who will trust us to do the job and do it right!

To get such a sensitive and far-seeing effort underway and so counter the present illogical and actually self-defeating clashes, arguments and prejudices between nations, all totally unscientific, the help of everyone interested is needed. Write to your congressmen and President with all the fervor you can command so the course of history can be changed towards reason and intelligence. We must convince the leaders of all nations that the present upward spiraling armaments race and its terrible waste of human and material resources is madness, and can lead only to world catastrophe. Arguments based mainly on emotion and ego must stop and be replaced by science and reason, also with compassion in the hearts of more leaders for all the life on this fragile planet, so that an intelligent solution of world problems can be arrived at. Understanding other nations is vital, especially the Russians, so we can work with them cooperatively. There are keys to the hearts nd minds of all peoples and we must find them!

The scientists themselves need to speak out more and more for an end of the absolute insanity of war and help devise ways to bring peace by multi-lateral and equally chorushed disarmament. Struggles, such as those in San Salvador and Guatemala, stem from lack of compassion of the rich and powerful for the poor of those lands. But compassion should not mean coddling the weak but instead strengthening them by training to become self-reliant. When compassion and science rule more and more hearts and minds, uspecially of our elected leaders, most of these barriers and conflicts between peoples will be overcome and be replaced by peace, freedom, justice, understanding and the scientific method. What a glorious day that will be!

[1] From page 148 of *The Russians And The Americans,* by Jules Archer. Hawtorn Books, 1975, by permission of the author.

X   Steps Toward A New Planetary Identity*

On How to Eliminate the Threat of Nuclear War

by Louis Rene Beres

"The storm...this storm you talk of... It will be such a one, my son, as the world has not seen before. There will be no safety by arms, no help from authority, no answer in science. It will rage till every flower of culture is trampled, and all human things are leveled in a vast chaos...The Dark Ages that are to come will cover the whole world in a single pall; there will be neither escape nor sanctuary."
High Lama in *Lost Horizon*

* * *

Today, this "storm" is not far off. It is almost upon us. As we go on and on with our seemingly important day-to-day concerns, the planet moves inexorably toward nuclear war. Just a few more years, perhaps, and there will remain no conceivable way of averting humankind's last paroxysm. The people of Earth will draw their last fitful, convulsive gasps. And they will do so, incredibly, with incredulity.

Although we have become used to such portentous omens during the past 35 years, the vision of a global nuclear wasteland must not be taken lightly. Our world is, after all, a grotesque distortion of humankind's vast potential for improvement; a hideous parody of what might have been. Teeming with the instruments of atomic destruction, it is a world with an ever-widening discrepancy between technical intelligence and reason. In such a world, one that has already been shaped by some 6,000 years of organized warfare, it is inconceivable that these instruments will remain dormant. Instead, the catastrophic possibilities that now lie latent in nuclear weapons are almost certain to be exploited, either by design or by accident, by misinformation or by miscalculation, by states or by subnational groups, by lapse from rational decision or by unauthorized decision.

To reverse this slide toward a nuclear Armageddon, three basic steps must be taken:

(1)General publics throughout the world must experience an aroused consciousness of the threat. Unless this threat is more widely understood, the existing momentum of interpersonal and international destructiveness will carry us forward toward irreversible despair. The hands on the *Bulletin's* doomsday clock advance steadily closer to midnight. We must recognize this movement before we can slow down its progress.

(2)A farreaching and feasible agenda for world order reform must be created. Such an agenda must represent the product of careful, well-reasoned, and imaginative scholarship. Although we still do not have the kind of World Peace Research Organization proposed by Nobel laureate Linus Pauling in his book, *No More War (1959)*, many scholars are currently seeking a way out of the global nuclear crisis. It must be their primary responsibility to shed light upon the implications of alternative courses of action. In so doing, they can begin to identify various blueprints for survival.

(3)We require the implementation of promising plans for world order reform. Once general publics have announced their concern and scholars have drawn up appropriate strategies, national leaders must begin to act. The time for "business as usual" in world politics has ended. Soon we must begin to construct a reliable ark of renewal—a global structure secure enough to deliver us all safely from the absurd drama of planetary political life. The stakes are the whole future of humankind.

Confronting the Threat. Our insistence upon facing the Gorgon Head of nuclear war is essential to success. It would be far more dangerous to approach the issue with an averted gaze. Only by trying to understand the full import of what such a war, in any of its conceivable forms, would mean for the countries involved, can we begin to take the required steps back toward a durable peace. Rather than turning us into stone, our unflinching look at the unthinkable can aid us in reversing the encroachment of worldwide atomic catastrophe. To do otherwise would be to accept the role of actors in a Greek tragedy who have lost command of their destinies, and who have forsaken the hope that human intervention can still be purposeful.

The motto for the eighteenth century period of enlightenment, *sapere aude!* (dare to know), suggested by the philosopher Kant, acquires a special meaning in the late twentieth century study of nuclear war. Just as repression of the fear of death by individuals can occasion activities that impair the forces of self-preservation, so can states impair their prospects for survival by insulating themselves from reasonable fears of collective disintegration. While it is true that the fear of death must be tempered in both individual and national drives lest it create paralysis, to deny the effect of such fear altogether is to make the threat of extinction more imminent.

If it is to serve any useful purpose, the fear generated by our straight forward look at the consequences of nuclear war must lead us away from that bloodless brand of realism that is so characteristic of strategic planners. Instead of rarefied think-tank analyses that reek of the very unreality they seek to dispel, we must begin to prevent nuclear war by highlighting its concrete human costs. Such euphemisms as "limited nuclear war," "collateral damage," "countervalue" and "counterforce" strategies and "enhanced radiation warfare" are dangerous to the cause of peace because they contribute to the myth that nuclear warfighting might be rational. To counter the strategic myth-makers, we must not only face the danger of nuclear war squarely, but prepare to rage against it with passion and partisanship.

Perhaps the closest we can come to understand what it really would be like to endure a nuclear conflict is by studying the anatomy of life in the death camps of Nazi Germany and the aftermath of atomic holocaust in Japan. Although the analogies are imperfect, there are no other darkly visionary sources of human experience to which we can so safely turn. The total immersion in death; the olfactory stimulation provided by tens of thousands of burning bodies; the overwhelming imagery of unending terror, disintegration and loss that were the central features of these two atrocities offer us the clearest human picture of life in a post-apocalypse world.

At the time of their descent into hell, the survivors of Auschwitz and Hiroshima, of Treblinka and Nagasaki, reacted to the otherworldy grotesqueness of their conditions with what Yale psychiatrist Robert J. Lifton describes as a profound sense of "death in life." Witness, in the one case, the thrusting of newly-delivered babies, alive, into ovens and, in the other, the appearance of long lines of severly burned, literally melting ghosts. The survivors found themselves, in Bruno Bettelheim's words, an "anonymous mass," or in the Japanese term, *maga-muchu,* "without self, without a center." Such a total disruption of individual and social order, of one's customary personal and community supports, produced consequences that went far beyond immediate physical and emotional suffering. Indeed, this understanding is incorporated in the Japanese term for atomic bomb survivors. *Hibakusha,* which delimits four categories of victims, including those who were *in utero* at the time of the blast.

Of course, in the case of nuclear war, the symbols and images needed to interpret the idea of total extinction simply do not exist. Their absence makes it impossible for us, in thinking about such war, to follow Martin Buber's injunction to "imagine the real." Nevertheless, even if a world numbed by nuclear apocalypse is not psychologically absorbable at the moment, imagining it must be encouraged.

In the unsentimental theater of modern world politics, the time is at hand for a new kind of dramaturgy, a new naturalism that touches profoundly the deepest rhythms of human imagination. Our playgoing sensibilities must no longer be confined to the implausible pap of "balance of terror," "successful nuclear deterrence," and "peace through strength." We require honest passages off down-to-earth exposition, even if the necessary tracts and tirades become endless and unbearable.

At the same time, we must resurrect the traditional function of theater to evoke pity and terror. The world is pregnant with apocalyptic possibilities. These possibilities must be acknowledged forthrightly. To witness the birth of a new world politics, a gravedigger must wield the forceps.

* * *

An Agenda for World Order Reform. How are we to stop the lemming-like march toward nuclear war? We live in a global society fraught with incentives to states to acquire or enlarge nuclear arsenals. These incentives include *presumed* advantages in terms of deterrence and international status as well as bolstered domestic political support, increased strategic autonomy, and leverage over major world powers. Unless states can be persuaded that these incentives are outweighed by a compelling array of disincentives, an extinctive outcome seems likely.

To accomplish such persuasion, steps must be taken to satisfy two interrelated objectives: a strenghtened tapestry of international treaties and agreements directed at non-proliferation, arms control and disarmament: and a generalized renunciation of the long-discredited principles of *realpolitik*. These steps rest upon the understanding that a working peace system demands not only customary restraints under international law, but also a full-fledged transformation of foreign policy processes. The creative apogee of such a cosmopolitan thinking can be reached only when all states learn to identify their own best interests with the security of the entire system of world politics.

The existing balance of terror between the superpowers cannot last indefinitely. At one point or another, for one reason or another, the strategy of peace through nuclear deterrence will fail. The alleged rationality of Mutually Assured Destruction (MAD) notwithstanding, this strategy—which is now being further undermined by counterforce targeting doctrines and by renewed preparation for active and passive defense—promises only temporary reprieve. What is to be done?

At one level, the answer is obvious. We must put an end to the nuclear arms race, especially the stepped-up development of new generations of strategic weapons. And ultimately, we must attempt the staged destruction of existing stockpiles of strategic nuclear weapons. Such staged destruction should be initiated by the superpowers and imitated progressively by other nuclear weapon states.

At another level, we must transform the characteristic behavior of the superpowers in world politics. We must create the conditions whereby the United States and the Soviet Union consider cooperation in the world interest to be in their respective national interests. While such a proposal must appear particularly fanciful, there is no other way. Only a joint understanding that the principles of *realpolitik* are strikingly unrealistic can offer enduring peace between the superpowers. Only a mutual renunciation and reversal of the long-cherished pattern of nuclear arms competition can give palpable form to the benefits of arms control and disarmament measures.

To provide meaningful arms control and disarmament, steps must be taken on four concrete, interrelated proposals:

(1)*Minimum deterrence.* The United States and the Soviet Union must retreat from their increasing acceptance of counterforce principles and return to the relative sanity of strategies based on minimum deterrence, that is, strategies based upon the ability to inflict an unacceptable degree of damage upon the aggressor after absorbing a nuclear first strike. It is widely understood that each side has this ability right now, and that each can continue to have such an ability without further deployment of nuclear weapons and with substantial reductions in existing arsenals. Since the survival of even the smallest fraction of American or Russian ICBMS, bombers and submarines could assure the destruction of the other, we now have perceptible levels of "overkill." And no conceivable breakthrough in military technology can alter this condition.

To facilitate the return to minimum deterrence, the superpowers must cooperate in the creation of a more harmonious pattern of interaction, a pattern that discourages both adventurism and risk-taking. This would mean immediate Senate ratification of SALT II; and end to the threatened deployment of particle beams as anti-satellite weapons because they would threaten the technical means of verifying SALT II; a joint reversal of current trends toward increased military spending; a slow-down in the international arms trade; and a reaffirmation of the spirit and principle of detente. Taken together, these policies could provide a new syntax of Soviet-American strategic relations, replacing short-sighted movements toward Cold War II with more enduring patterns of safety.

(2)*A Comprehensive test ban.* The time is at hand for banning all nuclear weapons testing—a comprehensive test ban. Notwithstanding the 1963 Partial Test Ban Treaty. the 1974 Treaty on the Limitation of Underground Nuclear Weapon Tests (also known as the Threshold Test Ban Treaty), the 1976 Treaty on Underground Nuclear Explosions for Peaceful Purposes, and the SALT II Protocol provisions dealing with flight testing of ICBMS, new types of ballistic missiles and certain kinds of cruise missiles, only a comprehensive test ban can substantially inhibit further nuclear weapon innovations. To be genuinly promising, a comprehensive test ban—which would be the culmination of a goal first outlined in the late 1950s—must include a moratorium on peaceful nuclear explosion tests, because these tests are effectively indistinguishable from nuclear weapons tests.

(3)*No-first-use pledge.* The United States and the Soviet Union must follow the example of China and take the declaratory step of renouncing the first use of nuclear weapons. Regrettably, although a no-first-use pledge would be an important first step in "delegitimizing" nuclear weapons, the superpowers continue to evade it. For the United States, this evasion stems from NATO strategy of deterring Soviet conventional attack with nuclear weapons and is reinforced by fears of American conventional force inferiority in Southwest Asia, the Middle East and Persian Gulf region.

Clearly, from the standpoint of current policy, a no-first-use pledge would be contrary to the central features of American nuclear deterrence strategy. To allow for a credible renunciation of the first-use option, the United States must undertake far-reaching efforts to strengthen conventional force capabilities, avoiding deployment of enhanced radiation weapons which would blur the distinction between nuclear and non-nuclear forces. Only then could it move confidently toward the abandonment of plans for a new generation of NATO intermediate-range missiles, the redeployment of theater nuclear forces away from all frontiers, and the ultimate removal of these forces altogether. And only then could we expect a credible no-first-use pledge by the Soviet Union.

(4)*Nuclear weapon free zones.* The superpowers must supplement their no-first-use pledge with an effective arrangement for nuclear weapon free zones. The concept of such zones has already received international legal expression in the Treaty for the Prohibition of Nuclear Weapons in Latin America (The Treaty of Tlatelolco), which entered into force on April 22, 1968, and the two additional Protocols to the Treaty. Unlike two earlier treaties which seek to limit the spread of nuclear weapons into areas yet to be contaminated—the Antarctic Treaty of 1961 and the Outer

Space Treaty of 1967—the Latin American Treaty concerns a populated area. The terms of the Treaty include measures to prevent the type of deployment of nuclear weapons that led to the Cuban missile crisis, methods of verification by both parties themselves and by their own regional organization, and International Atomic Energy Agency safeguards on all nuclear materials and facilities under the jurisdiction of the parties.

The present non-proliferation regime is founded upon a scaffolding of mutilated agreements, statutes and safeguards. It should be clear that proliferation would be inimical to the security of every state, even if the superpowers fail to live up to their Non-Proliferation Treaty obligation to curtail their own competition in strategic arms. Non-weapon states, however, hold to a different view. As they see it, a "bargain" has been struck between the superpowers and themselves, and unless the former begin to take more ambitious steps toward vertical arms control and disarmament, they, too, will move in the direction of strategic capability. Ironically but understandably, the non-weapon states consider this bargain to be the most prudent path to security.

What this means, from the standpoint of controlling nuclear proliferation, is that the superpowers must restructure their central strategic relationship with particular reference to SALT. It is imperative that SALT II be ratified soon, and that steps be taken to proceed to SALT III. The sorely misconceived policy of linkage, which ties support of SALT to the good behavior of the Soviet Union, must be discarded.

Together with other nuclear powers, the superpowers must also contribute to the belief that proliferation would be unattractive by enhancing the security of non-nuclear weapons states in other ways. A pledge by the nuclear powers not to use nuclear weapons against nonweapon states would be especially welcome. With the seating of China at the 1980 session of the Committee on Disarmament, that Committee should assume a more influential role in producing such a pledge. To the extent that such a pledge would be widely believed, it could contribute to the understanding that non-acquisition of nuclear weapons promotes safety.

To decouple civilian nuclear energy programs from the spread of nuclear weapons, major steps must be taken to strengthen both national and international institutions and procedures concerning the protection of nuclear facilities, materials and weapons-grade nuclear fuel. Pursuant to the report of the International Nuclear Fuel Cycle Evaluation, efforts must be made to ensure that the growing utilization of commercial nuclear power is not in the nature of a Faustian bargain—in other words, that it is not accompanied by the spread of nuclear weapons.

The core of these efforts must be a comprehensive non-proliferation regime highlighted by the Non-Proliferation Treaty. To make the treaty work successfully in the future, a number of changes are called for. These center on two elements of the treaty which persistently raise the greatest objections: those inherently discriminatory features which place an unequal set of obligations on non-nuclear weapon states; and the inherently weak safeguards systems. The first set of objections is usually raised by the non-nuclear weapon states, who feel that the treaty provides neither effective guarantees for their security nor reliable access to the energy benefits of nuclear power. The second set of objections is typically associated with the nuclear weapons states, who fear that the treaty provides too few meaningful constraints to halt proliferation.

The effectiveness of the non-proliferation regime will also depend upon nuclear export policy. Since access to a nuclear weapons capability may depend upon the policies of a small group of supplier states, such policies constitute a vital element of non-proliferation efforts. In the years ahead, those states that carry on international trade in nuclear facilities, technology and materials will have to improve and coordinate their export strategies.

Finally, to accomplish the objectives of non-proliferation, it is not enough to provide the customary restraints offered by treaties and institutions. Although such restraints are essential, they must be surrounded by a new field of consciousness—one that flows from a common concern for the human species and from the undimmed communion of individual states with the entire system of states.

Living at this juncture between world order and global disintegration, states must slough off the shackles of outmoded forms of self-interest. With the explosion of the myth of realism, the global society of states could begin to come together in a renewed understanding of the connection between survival and relatedness. When this happens, states will finally consummate their search for planetization.

Implementing a Plan for World Order Reform. The foregoing proposals constitute a coherent strategy for preventing nuclear war. Instead of simply fine-tuning overworked scenarios of nuclear gamesmanship, these proposals point toward a widespread disengagement from current patterns of strategic competition. Indeed, they comprise the essential elements of a promising "nuclear regime"—a system of obligations, force structures and doctrinal postures, based upon certain values and goals, and shaped by justifiably fearful expectations of the future.

However, something else is needed. Without necessarily seeking fundamental changes in the prevailing state-centric structure of global authority, the two superpowers must learn to associate their own security from nuclear war with a more farreaching search for worldwide stability and equity. To prevent nuclear war between the superpowers, the prescribed nuclear regime must be augmented by a new awareness of the "connectedness" of states.

Ultimately, the chances for a successful detachment from strategic arms competition will depend upon the specific steps needed to underscore the total disutility of a nuclear threat system. Implementation of these steps will require an early world summit of leaders from both rich and poor states, a summit of the sort recommended recently by the Brandt Commission Report to deal with international development issues. and these steps will depend upon a prior understanding, by the superpowers, that their own security interests are inevitably congruent with the security interests of the world as a whole. The balance of power between the Soviet Union and the United States can never be more stable than the balance of power in the whole of international society.

To prevent nuclear was that might occur through proliferation requires a nuclear regime that extends the principles of superpower war avoidance to the rest of international society. The centerpiece of this universal regime must be the cosmopolitan understanding that all states, like all people, form one essential body and one true community. Such an understanding, that a latent oneness lies buried beneath the manifold division of our fractioned world, need not be based on the mythical attractions of universal brotherhood and mutual concern. Instead, it must be based on the idea that individual states, however much they may dislike each other, are tied together in the struggle for survival. Will it work? Can humankind be expected to grasp this calculus of potentiality, reaffirming the sovereignity of reason over the forces of disintegration? Can states be expected to tear down the walls of competitive power struggles and replace them with the permeable membranes of spirited cooperation?

Perhaps not! But there is surely no other way. So long as individual states continue to identify their own security with the acquisition of destructive weaponry they will have only war. The Talmud tells us, "The dust from which the first man was made was gathered in all the corners of the world." By moving toward a new planetary identity, the peoples of Earth can begin to build bridges over the most dangerous abyss they have ever known. Hopefully, even in this absurd theater of modern world politics, human beings will choose life rather than death. Stripped of false hopes, and without illusion, man may yet stare at the specter of nuclear apocalypse with passionate attention and experience the planetary responsibility that will bring liberation.

*This essay appeared in The Bulletin of the Atomic Scientists 43, February 1981. Reprinted by permission of the Bulletin of the Atomic Scientists, a magazine of science and public affairs. Copyright© 1981.

XI   The Nuclear Solution *
Giving Up the Plutonium Security Blanket

by Dr. Roger Fisher

Dr. Roger Fisher, a professor of law at Harvard and an internationally recognized authority on negotiations theory, addressed these remarks to a group of doctors gathered for a conference on "The Medical Consequences of Nuclear Weapons and Nuclear War" sponsored by Physicians for Social Responsibility. As his talk makes clear, the "responsibility" falls to us all.

* * *

As I was getting ready to speak at this conference several people commented on my place at the end of the program. After two days on the results of nuclear disaster, I was scheduled to tell, in forty-five minutes, how to prevent it. A typical remark was, "Boy, have you got a problem!"

Whenever I hear that phrase I am reminded of a small incident that occurred during World War II. I was a B-17 weather reconnaissance officer. On one particularly fine day we were in Newfoundland test-flying a new engine. Our pilot took us up to about 14,000 feet and then, to give the new engine a rigorous test, he stopped the other three and feathered their propellers into the wind. We flew along on one engine for a few minutes. It is impressive to see what a B-17 can do on one engine. It cannot quite hold its altitude, but if it is light, it can do quite well. Then, just for a lark, the pilot feathered the fourth and last propeller and turned off the engine.

Suddenly the sound was gone. With all four propellers stationary, we glided, somewhat like a stone, toward the rocks and forests of Newfoundland. After a minute or so the pilot pushed the button to unfeather. Then he remembered to unfeather the propeller you had to have electrical power, and to have power you had to have at least one engine going. As we were buckling on our parachutes, the co-pilot burst out laughing. Turning to the pilot, he said, "Boy oh boy, have you got a problem!"

Like the crew of the B-17, we are all in this together. Yet I sense a tendency among us to put the problem of preventing nuclear war on someone else's agenda, though, we are all on board one fragile spacecraft, and the risk is high. What can we do to reduce it?

The problem is not just in the hardware. The problem lies in the way we think about nuclear weapons and in our working assumptions. If the problem lies in the way we think, then that is where the answer lies. In Pogo's immortal phrase, "We have met the enemy and they are us."

DANGEROUS ASSUMPTION #1: The Goal is to "Win"

The danger of nuclear war is so great primarily because of the mental box we have put ourselves in. We all have working assumptions which we take for granted and usually leave unexamined. It is these assumptions which make the world so dangerous. Three of them concern: (1) our ultimate goals —the ends we are pursuing; (2) the means for pursuing those ends; and (3) whose job it is to do what.

First, about our goals. Internationally (as well as nationally and politically) we think we want to "win". The assumption that victory is what we want is widespread. A story will illustrate the point.

In the late 1950s I spent two years in the Solicitor General's Office arguing cases for the government in the Supreme Court. I started off with an excellent batting average — eight wins and no losses — which made me really impossible to put up with. Oscar Davis, who was then First Assistant, said something to me then that I have always remembered: "You know, we don't want to win them all." I said, "Excuse me?" He said, "Did you ever think what would happen if the government of the United States won all the cases in the Supreme Court? Prosecutors would run amok, respect for the court would disappear, the whole concept of government under law would be destroyed—it would be a disaster."

I said, "But Oscar, what am I doing up there? I put on my striped trousers and my morning coat, I go up, I argue. What is the purpose?"

"Oh" he said, "we want to win each case, but not every case."

Internally as well as domestically, we need a system in which we can play to win, but not in which any one side — even our own — wins all the time.

In fact, like a poker player, we have three kinds of objectives. One objective is to win the hand. Whatever it is we think we want, we want it now: We want victory. The second objective is to be in a good position for future hands. We want a reputation and chips on the table so that we can influence future events. We want power. Our third objective is not to have the table kicked over or the house burned down while we are playing. We want peace.

We want victory, we want power, and we want peace. And exploding nuclear weapons will not help us achieve any one of them. We have to reexamine rigorously our working assumption that in a future war we would want to "win".

NATIONAL SECURITY: We're Safe Only If They Are

We also need to re-examine our self-centered definition of national security. Typically, political leaders suggest that the first issue of foreign policy is national security and only after that has been taken care of should we worry about our relations with the Soviet Union, China, and other countries. Such thinking assumes that somehow we can be secure while the Soviet Union is insecure. But missiles fly both ways. There is no way we can make the world more dangerous for them without also making it more dangerous for ourselves. If their end of the boat tips over, we all drown.

I may point out that those of us who preach such things frequently do not practice what we preach. I am always prepared to tell my friends at the Pentagon that it does no good to call the Soviets idiots. "Don't you see that, you idiot?" I say. We who are concerned with reducing the risks of war frequently think our job is to "win" the war against hawks. In worrying about the war against hawks, we often assume that our adversaries have no side worth considering. To the contrary. We have to find out what their legitimate concerns are, and we have to solve their legitimate interests in order to solve our own. At every level, we need to re-examine our objectives. We are not seeking to win a war, but to gain a peace.

DANGEROUS ASSUMPTION #2: Security Comes From Force

The second set of dangerous assumptions are those we make about means — about how to pursue our objectives.

If there is a problem, we will first try diplomacy. But if that doesn't solve the problem we assume we can use force. The reality, however, is that the big problems in today's world have no military solution. Nuclear war is not a solution. It is worse than any problem it might "solve". There is no way we can make the world work by using nuclear bombs. It cannot be done. The only means we have is to try to change somebody's mind.

SEEING THINGS AS OTHERS SEE THEM

We all know far better ways to deal with international problems:

- Break up big problems into manageable pieces. Look at each item on its merits.
- Sit down with the other side and discuss the problem.
- Don't concentrate on what people say their positions are, but try to understand and deal with their interests.
- Communicate and, in particular, listen. What's on their mind? What's bothering them? Before we can change their minds, we have to know where their minds are. We have to put ourselves in their shoes. The only way we can reduce the threat of war is to affect their future thinking. The starting point is to understand their present thinking.

Next, we have to invent wise solutions. We have to find good ways to reconcile our differing interest. Both sides must participate in that process. There is no way in any conflict for one side by itself to produce the right answer. The understanding that comes from working jointly on a problem, and the acceptability that comes from having participated in creating a solution, both make any good answer better.

The same process applies equally in dealing with our domestic differences. Again, those of us who want disarmament are not the only source of wisdom. We are part of the conflict. There are many people in this country who have legitimate concerns about the Soviet Union. We have got to put ourselves in their shoes — Pentagon shoes — just as we ask them to put themselves in ours.

Neither of us should insist on inventing all the answers ourselves. We must all participate, not carry on a war.

In this process we will need to promote joint problem-solving not just at the intellectual level but at the level of feeling, at the level of emotion, the level of caring, the level of concern. International conflict is too often dealt with cerebrally, as though it were a hypothetical problem. We need to apply what we know, and, even more, keep on learning about human behavior. We want to understand how to affect it, not just manipulate it — to realign the forces within us to work in a better direction.

DANGEROUS ASSUMPTION #3: It's Someone Else's Job

The danger of nuclear war also comes from a third set of assumptions about whose job it is to reduce the risk of war.

If there were a military solution, there would be a case for leaving it to the military, to policy-science experts, and to professional strategists. But we are not facing a technical military problem.

The solution lies within each of us, in changing our assumptions — and in changing other people's assumptions. The solution lies in reaching maturity, in abandoning our plutonium security blanket.

There is no one I know who has a professional license in the skills of reducing the risk of nuclear war. Fortunately, no professional license is required. But who has the skills to deal with psychological problems like denial, like turning flesh-and-blood issues into abstract problems through the use of jargon? Who is likely to notice people deny responsibility because a problem seems overwhelming? Weapons engineers? I think not.

Earlier, I left you in a B-17 over the hills of Newfoundland. Our co-pilot was telling the pilot that he had a problem. Well, we didn't crash. We weren't all killed. On that plane we had a buck sergeant who remembered that back behind the bomb bay we had a putt-putt generator in case we landed at some emergency air field that did not have electric power to start the engines. He ran back, fiddled with the carburetor, wrapped a rope around the flywheel a few times, pulled it and pulled it, got the generator going, and before we were down to 3,000 feet we had electricity. The pilot could restart the engines, and we were all safe. Saving that plane was not the sergeant's job in the sense that the danger was his fault or responsibility. But it was his job in the sense that he had an opportunity to do something about it.

My notion of whose job something is, is best defined by who has an opportunity. We have an opportunity. I encourage you, as I encourage myself, to use it. The world is at risk. The very danger of nuclear war means that there is more opportunity for each of us to make a difference than ever.

COURSES OF ACTION: There's Plenty To Do

Look at the opportunities. Somebody has to propose a solution. Somebody has to put it on the public agenda. Somebody has to persuade others that it is a good idea, and somebody has to carry it out. There is enough to keep all of us busy. No single activity will be sufficient.

My first arms control proposal, almost twenty years ago, dealt with the problem of remoteness from reality that the President must have if he faces a decision about nuclear war. There is a young officer who follows the President with a black attache case containing the codes needed to fire nuclear weapons. I envisioned the President at a staff meeting considering nuclear war as an abstract question. He might conclude, "On SIOP Plan One, the decision is affirmative. Communicate the Alpha line XYZ." Such jargon holds the results of his action at a distance.

My suggestion was quite simple. Put the code number in a little capsule and implant the capsule right next to the heart of a volunteer. The volunteer would have a big, heavy butcher knife to carry as he or she accompanied the President. If ever the President wanted to fire nuclear weapons and kill tens of millions of people, he would have to start by killing one human being, personally. The President would have to look at a human being and realize what death is — what an innocent death is. Blood on the White House carpet. Reality brought home. When I suggested this to friends in the Pentagon, they said, "My God, that's terrible! Having to kill someone would distort his judgment. The President might never push the button."

Whether or not this particular idea has any merit, there is much to do. People often tell me, "I don't know what to do." That gives you something to do right there. Get a half-dozen friends together next Saturday morning and figure out some things you might do. Identify three or four other people who you think might make decisions of some significance. What are some of those decisions? Why haven't they made them already? What can you do to increase the chance they'll make some desired decision next week? Whoever it is — journalists, people in government, businesspeople, civic organizations, professional societies, a friend of President Reagan — what are some things they might do that would illuminate our faulty working assumptions and help establish better ones? Figuring out what to do is itself a good thing to do. In intellectual efforts, as in gunnery, one's aim is crucial.

Don't wait to be instructed. Think for yourself. This is not an organized campaign that someone else is going to run. If you share these concerns, get involved. The security blanket most of us cling to is, "Don't blame me. It's not my job to plan nuclear strategy. I'm not responsible for the risk of nuclear war. I told people they shouldn't have a nuclear war." You can give up that security blanket any time, beginning today.

The way we can enlist support is less to burden others with guilt than to provide them with an opportunity to volunteer. I find it a happy venture. It is a glorious world outside. The sun is shining. There are people to love and pleasures to share. Details of past wars and the threat of the future should not take away the fun and the joy we can have working together on a challenging task. I see no reason to be gloomy about acting to save the world. Be involved, not just intellectually, but emotionally. Here is a chance to work together with affection, with caring, with feeling. Let some of your emotions hang out a bit. We are human beings. Be human.

People have struggled all of their lives to clear ten acres of ground, or simply to maintain themselves and their families. Look at the opportunity we have. Few people in history have been given such a chance — a chance to apply our convictions, our values, our highest moral goals with such competence as our professional skills may give us. A chance to work with others — to have the satisfaction that comes from playing a role, however small, in a constructive enterprise. It's not compulsory. So much the better. But what challenge could be greater? We have an opportunity to improve the chance of human survival.

*By kind permission of Dr. Roger Fisher.

XIIA Let's Negotiate The Peace Of The World

by Vinson Brown

Almost all of us are negotiators at least some times in our lives. A man negotiates with his wife over what kind of house to buy. A boy negotiates with his sister as to what movie to see on TV. *But the most important negotiation in all history is the negotiation to bring genuine peace to the world. It is so important that if the negotiations for that Peace are successful and the earth is saved from war, the famous heroes of the past, such as the Greeks who held back the Persians at Thermopylae, Julius Caesar conquering Gaul and Rome, Columbus discovering the New World, and even Ghandi winning freedom for India from Britain, would pale into insignificance by comparison.* The names of these heroes of Peace will be sung down the centuries perhaps as long as human life is on this planet, for the gift they would give to humanity will be the most thrilling and vital the world has ever known and perhaps will ever know.

Yet there are some people who say such peace is impossible. They exclaim, "How can we possibly trust the Communists?" But they do not realize that, with what they think are equally good reasons the Communists say, "How can we ever trust the capitalist countries?" There is some reason for such mistrust on both sides. We remember how Castro pretended he was not a Communist and then became one when he came to power in Cuba. Russian Communists remember how President Eisenhower swore we were not sending spy planes over Russia, but then sheepishly admitted we had done so when the Russians shot down the spy plane of Gary Powers.

We can indeed convince other peoples to be trustworthy when we can show them graphically that their very lives and that of their children hang in the balance and that almost sure destruction will come to all of us if we do not wake up, grow up and bring the nations into harmony under International Law. It is true there are tremendous difficulties and that all negotiations may fail, but the smell of death is in the air these days and growing stronger. Millions are awakening to the overwhelming need for Peace and

understanding. Millions are no longer content with drifting help-
lessly into the most horrible war of all history, one that might
literally destroy our civilization. And at last the politicians are
beginning to listen. The time to strike for Peace has come!

I am going to suggest here briefly how we can negotiate with
the Russians and eventually all nations to bring peace to the
world. However, the steps I give here are not all mine but partly
what I have derived or absorbed from a very fine and powerfully
convincing book called *Getting To Yes, Negotiating Agreement Without
Giving In,* by Drs. Roger Fisher and William Ury, published by
Houghton Mifflin Co. of Boston Massachusetts in 1981. Though I
deeply appreciate their help and the permission of Houghton
Mifflin to use some of the words in the book in this essay, I wish to
state that the way I have shaped the ideas are mainly mine and are
not to be construed as reflecting exactly their concepts or feelings.
But I do suggest that you read their book for a fuller understanding of how to negotiate in general and particular. Both Fisher and
Ury are respectably Director and Assistant Director of the Harvard Negotiation Project, which is actively engaged in teaching
diplomats and others who need help these new and innovative
ideas for successful negotiations.

I   The Problem

We and other nations must face the problem that there is no
hope for a true and lasting peace for the world until the United
Nations is given enforceable power and world law to prevent war.
It is in the United Nations Constitution that the nations who are
members are joined together in this body to prevent war, but this
is an absolute farce and has no meaning until the present weak-
ness of the UN before the major powers is changed to strength.
Yet each of the great nations in the Security Council will probably
cling to its right to veto, like a baby to its security blanket, until all
grow big enough to see that they can have far better protection
from attack within a strong United Nations than through their
present go-it-alone approach. The principle involved is Peace
through United Strength, with each nation totally giving up its
right to go to war. At the same time each nation will be guaranteed
through a strong United Nations Constitution, signed by all, that
it will be allowed control over the interior affairs of its own

country as long as it does not practice genocide or other unlawful cruelties to innocent citizens and does not go to war with other nations. Obviously most nations are not ready yet for this big step, but there are signs they are awakening and will soon listen to intelligent negotiation.

II The Method — Intelligent Negotiation

A. *Don't bargain over positions.* The U.S., for example, claims it will not agree to a nuclear freeze until it is sure it has parity with the Russians to nuclear weapons. This position is so absurd as to be ridiculous as either major power has enough H bombs and the means to throw them so as to come near pulverzing the other. The Russians show a similarly absurd attitude when they say they will allow only very limited inspections of their armaments by U.N. Observers. Both nations must put the principle of peace first and strive to find ways to bring it about.

1. This is done partly by separating the people from the problem, by getting them away from rigid positions and get them to see each others views on peace and how it can be accomplished. Positions create rigid emotional stances that cause negotiations to fail. Let's leave them alone!

2. We must have perception of other people as thinking, feeling human beings and try to see and feel their thoughts by putting ourselves in their shoes, which brings intelligent understanding. We must make proposals that draw in their need for security and how it can be created by strengthening the U.N.

3. We can keep emotions under control by understanding their emotions and allowing them to emote if they wish, while remaining calm and reasonable ourselves. Absolutely no backbiting must be practiced!

4. We can communicate best by listening intently to what they have to say and understanding it, causing them to feel we understand their side and their ideas.

5. Be friendly, even use jokes, but get them to face problems and principles constructively so as to find reasonable solutions.

6. Get teamwork into the working for peace by getting the other side to work with us intelligently on problems and their solving.

B. *Reconcile interests between nations by developing ideas for mutual gain.*

1. Define the problem of peace and how it will help end poverty and unemployment as well as war if used constructively.

2. Ask questions and ask them to ask questions on how and why peace must work to make the nations whole and cooperating with each other.

3. After listening, explain how you understand their ideas, but be always ready to say, "Correct me if I am wrong!" This will disarm them and create confidence in your fairness and open-mindedness.

4. Build your own interest in peace to white heat so that others can feel the thrill you feel about it. This may create in them a desire to be a part of a very exciting adventure, especially if you draw their ideas on peace into the discussion and make them lively.

5. Brainstorm with your side and the other sides to find new ideas for bringing peace to the world. This is part of the scientific method, trying every avenue of approach you can think of until you find the ones that work best. If you can get the other side to brainstorm with you, a feeling of mutual trust, interest and understanding should grow. You can then pinpoint and emphasize the ideas that give signs of really working to break down the walls between nations.

6. Make a circle chart to help dramatize this, with the first step the problem (peace or war) in the real world. Second is the analysis (in theory) of the problem, its causes and the ways to resolve it. Third comes many possible approaches, strategies and cures, all combining into broad ideas of what can be done. Fourth comes putting the ideas into action, especially through strengthening the United Nations, and developing the first and then final steps for complete disarmament except for security police forces for each nation, and with a major police force in the United Nations to prevent conflict, plus a World Court to judge equitably between the nations.

7. If the opposing party or parties in the negotiation resort to any form of trickery, such as camouflaging their designs as in the interests of peace, when actually they are trying to weaken the United States, or others, while trying to preserve and increase military superiority for their side, this calls for the utmost firmness and wisdom to handle. They must be shown over and over until they thoroughly understand that world peace demands absolutely equal disarmament by all the major powers, plus full

rights for the United Nations, and any nation that feels threatened, to carefully inspect all armed forces or armaments that exist in any nation that is under suspicion, and that the United Nations has the full right to keep such armed forces and armaments to the limit agreed to by international treaty so that no nation can build up its arms to start another war.

C. *In all areas insist on objective criteria and courtesy* before and during the making of decisions. This can best be done by letting several well known scientists from all sides take part in the deliberations, letting them show how the scientific method can keep ideas and deliberations on a firm footing of fact and away from too much emotion and bad feelings. Let everybody remember and be reminded that the fate of the whole human race is involved. For the sake of billions of people and endless generations to come the nations must agree on a sensible and practical way to end war. Intelligence, science, courtesy, understanding and compassion must be used to bring this about. Never can it be done if there is too much emotion, prejudice, fear or hate.

XIIB Understanding the Russians

by Vinson Brown

A review of, *The Nuclear Delusion, Soviet American Relations in the Atomic Age,* by George Kennan, Pantheon Books, New York, in 1982.

The extremely vital nature of this book to America and to all the world is that it gives to us the wonderfully keen and well-balanced views of probably the outstanding American expert on Russia and Russian-American relations, explaining these relations and how we can avoid a suicidal war. The danger always in great crises in world history is that people, including even famous leaders, make serious mistakes in judgment, due partly to emotional conditioning or emotional reactions, but also through failure to diagnose the problem or problems with the necessary balance and wisdom, essentially to fail to use the scientific method, which attacks a difficult problem from all sides with equal vigilance and thoroughness.

George Kennan uses this vigilance and points out that a climate of mutual suspicion and misunderstanding between Russia and the United States has created such a dark cloud of equal antagonism that the two great nations are rushing towards an explosion so horrible and yet so stupidly futile that the world as a whole has never been in such danger. All the earth and its helpless children, almost all life also, would be endangered because of the immense power and ecologic consequences of an all-out hydrogen bomb war, which could be more terrible and wide-spread than even our scientists are able to determine.

Kennan makes very clear, though, that this is an artificial

condition brought on by human blindness and can be remedied if we begin to use our intelligence and wisdom instead of emotion, hate and misunderstanding. For example, he points out that while we could consider Stalin a monster because of what he did so ruthlessly to millions of his own people in the 1930's, the Russian leadership since that time has become much more reasonable, and handles its dissidents far more kindly than during Stalin's days of terror. But he also points out that those American leaders who constantly attack the Russians in their words and in their threats of building bigger and bigger nuclear and other armaments, are actually driving the Russian leaders to become more and more suspicious of us and threatening in their turn. He shows how this dreadful downhill advance towards inevitable conflict can be reversed if we understand the Russian leaders and their people more keenly, realizing their limitations, but also finding ways to convince them of the far greater benefits for both countries and for the world if peace comes. Despite contrary opinion, he claims these Russian leaders are not out to conquer the world, but are men who react too strongly to the fear that we wish to destroy them, which in turn builds up the suspicions on our side.

It is true that the Russians, under Stalin, after World War II, kept up their armaments and vast armies even when the United States and other countries were disarming. It is true that the Russians today are difficult to deal with because of their suspicions of capitalist countries and other prejudices. But Kennan urges us to understand the causes of this. For example, *Russians were victims over a period of eight centuries of not less than six different invasions of their country by outsiders who were very destructive and terrifying.* First were Genghis Khan and his Mongols, then the Tartars of the Golden Horde, the Poles, the Swedes, the French under Napoleon, and very recently and worst of all the Germans under Hitler. It is no wonder they suffer from a fearful view of the world, thinking somebody is out to get them!

Their attempts to spread Communism to other countries succeed only where these usually very poor countries have an upper class so vicious and exploitative in its actions that the poor people feel they have no way out except to revolt. Where true democracy exists, with human rights honored and the secret ballot for voting prevails, the Communists completely fail.

Because of their suspicion and fear, however, the Russians are very dangerous, which means we must deal with them with the utmost tact, care and firmness, but at the same time use friendliness and great wisdom to finally overwhelmingly convince them that multilateral disarmament, carefully monitored by the United Nations and with full inspection of the process, will bring them far greater protection against invasions and give them infinitely better conditions for their people than any possible war or any continued fantastic and unwise build-up of armaments as is happening today.

Kennan's explanation of all this is superb. In short, this is a book that is a prime necessity for every awake and plenty of unawake human beings to read, and then join in the mighty and vital struggle to prevent a holocaust before it is too late!

Epilogue

And when we have PEACE at last, what then? *Then the struggle continues,* that all nations, under God, shall enjoy liberty and justice for all, and that, as Abraham Lincoln so nobly, but partly, put it at Gettysburg in 1864: "Government of the people, by the people, and for the people shall" *spread to the whole earth.*

Then let us also remember his other words at his Second Inaugural — immortal words that apply to the situation today as much as they did to the situation then: (Note: I have just slightly, as above, changed a little of his wording.)

"With malice toward none, with charity for all, with firmness in the right, as God gives us to see the right, let us strive to finish the work we are in, to bind up *the nations'* wounds, to care for him who shall have borne the battle, and for his widow and orphans: to do all which may achieve a just and lasting peace among ourselves and with all nations."